trotman

BROOKLANDS COLL[...]
HEATH ROAD, WEYBRIDGE [...]
Tel: (01932) 7[...]

D0491142

This item must be returned on [...]
entered below. Subject to certain conditions, the loan
period may be extended upon application to the Librarian

30/6/09

AUTHOR CAPREZ
TITLE Journalism uncovered
CLASSIFICATION NO. 790.023
ACCESSION NO. 102361

Journalism

UNCOVERED

edition

BROOKLANDS COLLEGE LIBRARY
102361

Journalism Uncovered

This second edition published in 2009 by Trotman Publishing,
a division of Crimson Publishing Ltd.,
Westminster House, Kew Road,
Richmond, Surrey TW9 2ND

© Trotman Publishing 2009

First edition published in 2003 by Trotman and Company Ltd.

Author Emma Caprez

British Library Cataloguing in Publication Data
A catalogue record for this book is available
from the British Library

ISBN 978 1 84455 172 9

All rights reserved. No part of this publication may be reproduced, stored in a retrieval system or transmitted in any form or by any means, electronic and mechanical, photocopying, recording or otherwise without prior permission of Trotman Publishing.

Typeset by RefineCatch Limited, Bungay, Suffolk

Printed and bound in Great Britain by
Athenaeum Press, Gateshead

CONTENTS

About The Author

Emma Caprez studied for her BA (hons) in Design and Media Management at Thames Valley University. For her final-year project she researched, wrote and illustrated a book on the history of the Ealing School of Art and organised a follow-up exhibition and reunion. She graduated with first-class honours in 1993. She has worked on several research projects, including one on the feasibility of drama therapy for disabled people and contributed towards university literature. She has written for two international music papers, *Rumba* and the *LA Rock Review* and has had photographs published in *Melody Maker*. Emma also wrote *Getting into the Media* (and produced the video of the same name) and *Getting into Performing Arts*, *Real Life Issues: Bullying*, *Real Life Guides: Care*, and edited *The Disabled Students' Guide to University*, all published by Trotman. Emma also wrote, *Tommy's Dad*, illustrated by Nick Sharratt, for Action For Prisoners' Families. She lives with her partner and two children in London.

Acknowledgements

Thank you so much to the contributors for giving their professional advice and experience: Mike Baess, Nicola Baird, Kathryn Batchelor, Jonathan Bethy, Jane Dreaper, Elizabeth Gobeski, Lizzie Hosking, Scott Manson, Sean McManus, Colin Meek, Bernie Menezes, Alan Morrison, Fiona Murray, Leon Neal, John Pullman, Alyson Rudd, Sadie Sheppard, Gilly Sinclair, Justine Trueman, Lorraine Davies, Gabriel Green, Dan Palmer, Anila Khanna, Judith Wilson, Laura Barnett and John Thompson.

A very big thank you to my mother, Arlette Caprez, and to Mandy Prowse.

Thanks also to the National Union of Journalists, the PPA, the Newspaper Society, journalism.co.uk and Skillset for allowing me to use the information they gleaned from their research (*Journalists at Work: A Survey of Journalists in the UK Audio-Visual and Publishing Industries*, Skillset/Publishing NTO, 2002); to Stewart Gillies at the British Library Newspaper Library.

And, of course, a huge thank you to my gorgeous daughters, BibaMaya and Sukyella – who make great investigative journalists themselves – and my wonderful partner, Rook, who is the most talented person I know. Big thanks also to the rest of my family, Peach and Maisie Kazen, Timo, Alex, Lukas and Kaiya Kaltio, Dicky Pool and Pops, as well as my family of friends, Lynn and Poppy Towers, Sophie Kviman, Linda and Simon Bryer, Adrian McKinney, James and Sarah Lawless, Jim Bishop, Claire Longstaff, Shay and Louise Leonard, Selina Hussein, Rachel Lewin, Phillip Hawker and all for their support.

Emma Caprez

Past to present

The following information about the history of the British newspaper between 1600 and 2007 is given by kind permission of the British Library Newspapers. Go to www.bl.uk/collections/britnews.html for further information.

1620 First Coranto newspaper in English published in Amsterdam.

1641 First reporting of Parliament.

1679 Lapse of Licensing Act brings a flood of unlicensed newspapers, which are later suppressed.

1693 *Ladies Mercury* founded, the first women's magazine.

1695 Parliament decides against renewing Licensing Act; the way is cleared for a free press.

1701 Probable date of first issue of *Norwich Post*, probably the first provincial newspaper.

1702 *Daily Courant* founded, the first daily paper.

1706 *Evening Post* founded, the first evening paper.

1709 First Copyright Act; *Tatler* founded.

1737 *Belfast Newsletter* founded, the world's oldest surviving general daily newspaper.

1747 *Aberdeen Journal* – later *Press and Journal* – founded, the oldest surviving Scottish newspaper.

1785 *Daily Universal Register* founded, which became *The Times* in 1788, Britain's oldest surviving newspaper with continuous daily publication.

1788 *Star and Evening Advertiser* launched, the first daily, evening newspaper.

1791 *Observer* founded, the oldest surviving Sunday newspaper.

1806 First use of illustration in *The Times*, of Nelson's funeral.

1822 *Bell's Life in London* adds '*and Sporting Chronicle*' to its title, the first newspaper to include sport as a major component.

1832 First recorded British newspaper cartoon, published in *Bell's New Weekly Messenger*.

1842 *Illustrated London News* launched, first fully illustrated weekly.

1844 First story based on telegraph news printed in *The Times*, birth of Queen's son at Windsor.

1851 Reuters News Agency opens in London.

1855 Repeal of Stamp Act opens the way for cheap, mass circulation newspapers and modern newspaper design in terms of spacing and headlines.

1868 Press Association formed.

1880 W T Stead succeeds John Morley on *Pall Mall Gazette* and introduces 'new journalism', including the interview and gossip column, into Britain.

1889 Earliest use of photography, of Cambridge and Oxford boat crews, in *Illustrated London News*.

1893 *Financial Times* first appears on pink paper.

1897 Largest news illustration ever printed by a daily paper in this country, of the Diamond Jubilee procession, published by the *Daily Mail*.

1900 *Daily Express* launched. First national daily to put news on the front page.

1903 *Daily Mirror* launched. First daily illustrated exclusively with photos.

1907 National Union of Journalists founded.

1915 'Teddy Tail', first British comic strip, published in the *Daily Mail*.

1924 First crossword in a British newspaper appears in the *Sunday Express*.

1934 *Daily Mail* publishes the first photo to be transmitted by beam radio (from Melbourne to London).

1953 General Council of the Press formed, replaced by the Press Council in 1964 and Press Complaints Commission in 1991.

1962 Launch of the *Sunday Times* magazine as the *Sunday Times Colour Section*.

1966 *The Times* begins printing news on the front page.

1969 Rupert Murdoch begins buying up newspapers, including the *Sun*, which he relaunches as a tabloid.

1980 *Daily Star* printed simultaneously by facsimile in London and Manchester.

1981 *Mail on Sunday* launched, the first photo-composed national newspaper in Britain.

1987 First women editors of national newspapers in modern times: Wendy Henry (*News of the World*) and Eve Pollard (*Sunday Mirror*).

1997 *Shetland Times* v *Shetland News*, Scotland's test case on internet links, permits the *Shetland News*, under certain conditions, to link to stories on the *Shetland Times*' website.

1999 *Metro* launched, a daily newspaper distributed free to travellers on the London Underground.

2000 Journalists increasingly writing for new media. The internet becomes the first source of breaking news as pages can be updated 24 hours a day. *Business am* launched, the first, new, daily newspaper in Scotland for 100 years.

2002 London Press Club celebrates tercentenary of the founding of the *Daily Courant*, the first Fleet Street daily newspaper, with a service at St Bride's Church attended by Prince Charles.

2003 September: *Independent* publishes tabloid-sized version concurrently with broadsheet version. Two months later *The Times* follows suit.

2004 *Independent* ceases to publish broadsheet version, now publishes tabloid-size only. *The Times* again follows suit six months later. *The Times* is the first newspaper to publish a sudoku puzzle. *Daily Mail* begins publishing them three days later. In December, *Standard Lite* is launched, free afternoon edition of the *Evening Standard*, distributed in central London. The forerunner of the *London Lite*.

2005 *City Am* launched, a business free-sheet distributed in the City of London. *Guardian* switches to 'Berliner' format.

2006 *Observer* switches to Berliner format. *First News* launched, a children's newspaper aimed at 9- to 12-year-olds. Newspaper Publishers Association celebrates its centenary with an exhibition at the British Library: 'Front page: celebrating 100 years of the British newspaper 1906–2006'. *London Lite* is launched, free paper from Associated Newspapers distributed to London commuters in the late afternoon/early evening. In direct competition, the *London Paper* is also launched, free paper from News International distributed to London commuters in the late afternoon/early evening.

2007 British Library announces plan to move its newspaper collection from Colindale to a new purpose-built storage facility by December 2012. Digital and microfilm access to the collection is to be provided at the Library's St Pancras site. Conrad Black, former owner of the *Daily Telegraph*, sentenced to six-and-a-half years in prison in USA for his role in the multi-million-dollar fraud at Hollinger International, the newspaper group he created and controlled.

CHAPTER 1

The brief

'Industry forecasts predict that by 2010 there will be between 80,000 and 90,000 journalists in the UK.'
Journalists at Work, Skillset/Publishing NTO, 2002

JARGON BUSTERS

- **Berliner format** newspaper format marginally taller and wider than tabloid format
- **Bliki** blog that can be edited and approved by users
- **Blog** online diary or commentary by one person that other people can add comments to
- **Body text** main text on a page
- **Breaking news** new story item
- **Copy** editorial matter including text and images
- **CSS** cascading style sheets: application to style web pages written in HTML and XHTML including colours, fonts and layout

- **Cyberjournalist** online journalist
- **Interactive strategies** methods used to bring about more interactivity with reader/viewer
- **Podcasts** free downloadable audio recordings
- **RSS** real simple synchronisation or syndication: news feeds of latest headlines and videos, fed straight to user's PC as soon as new content is published
- **Run** number of copies printed; or to publish a story
- **Scoop** exclusive story or first story to be published about a subject
- **Streaming** sending audio or video in real time to the end user
- **Traffic** number of users recorded visiting a website
- **Unique users** number of individual users to a website
- **Webcast** broadcasting sound and images on the internet.

WHY READ THIS BOOK?

Because you want to be a journalist and you need some helpful hints on how to get into the industry?

Once journalists were seen as sleazy characters, encroaching on people's privacy, but these days they and their constantly changing profession are generally regarded with more respect. Journalism is one of the top career choices for graduates and yet it doesn't always pay well. There's a huge amount of competition and a lot of hard work is involved – both in doing the job and trying to get one. It requires training, learning skills, gaining loads of work experience (unpaid of course) and lots and lots of determination and passion on your part. To top it off, it's not exactly the easiest profession to get into. Are you still up for it? Yes? Then read on, because this book provides you with top tips on training, work experience, organisations, applications, job information and plenty of really useful advice from people already working in the industry.

WHAT IS A JOURNALIST?

A journalist is someone who communicates information by words and/or pictures (still and moving) to a target audience via a number of different media: newspapers, magazines, radio, television, the internet, and new media platforms, such as emails, text-messaging and other digital formats.

The majority of journalists work for regional or local papers – print and now increasingly online versions – and these publications are usually the entry route for young people finding work in journalism. The more popular media – national newspapers, television and consumer magazines – are much harder to get into, and journalists usually only work in these sectors once they have established their careers in other areas, with experience and a good portfolio needed to guarantee them entry.

WHY JOURNALISM?

Journalists play an important part in disseminating information to the general public. This may be celebrity gossip, such as the ongoing personal problems of Amy Winehouse or Britney Spears; life-changing news, such as the American presidential elections; or facts people need to make an informed choice, for example about the impact of global warming and why we need to consume less and recycle more.

If you want to work in newspapers, however, your first job will most probably be as a general news reporter for a local newspaper, covering a specific geographical area, where you might deal with anything from golden wedding anniversaries to murder and scandal.

OVERVIEW OF THE INDUSTRY

The advent of digital technologies has had a massive impact on traditional print and broadcast media, opening up new and exciting opportunities for journalists. Internet journalism is a huge global development creating a world where access to public information has been thrown wide open to both the producer and the consumer.

Since the first edition of *Journalism Uncovered*, the emergence, development and take-up of new technologies and digital platforms has dramatically affected the world we live in, how we conduct our lives and not least the way news and information is disseminated. Once the dominion of print and broadcast, the delivery of news has now been superseded by the internet and digital technologies in terms of our access to it, the way we receive it and the immediacy of the information it brings us, in particular breaking news. Digital platforms can deliver news 24 hours a day with stories updated for a global audience every minute, and with the increased connectivity of the internet brought about by the wide availability of broadband, this type of news can be very easily accessed by millions of people around the world every day.

As with the introduction of anything new, the delivery of news on the internet has brought about a knock-on effect to traditional media. Newspaper and many magazine sales have nosedived. Annual regional and national newspaper figures show that circulation is steadily declining.

For many, particularly the younger audience, the internet is the primary source for receiving news and finding out what's going on, not just locally, but nationally and internationally as well. Once shunned by print and broadcast media, news publishing industries can no longer ignore the power of the internet. Indeed, the capabilities of distributing news and information via the internet have brought about exciting challenges to news publishers who have had to look beyond print if they are to engage a larger, global audience.

With the internet capable of reaching a global audience, website versions of national newspapers grab viewers by covering stories that will attract as much traffic as possible – the more traffic, the greater the chance of selling advertising space to fund the online edition. This has caused concern that less attention-grabbing news isn't getting covered. Big stories get big traffic on a national and international scale. Many of the national newspaper websites attracted a huge traffic of unique users when they covered the story of the death of Heath Ledger in January 2008, and then traffic dipped (although still remaining high compared with print versions of the paper) in February, when there were fewer show-biz stories to divulge.

It's not just the national newspapers that have had to respond to the power of digital technologies. The UK regional press is increasing its local markets and audiences across an expanding portfolio of websites, niche magazines and broadcast platforms.

With the internet has also come increased interactivity. Now readers can comment on news stories and indeed provide them. Viewers are also sharing their mobile phone stills and video footage of news items on internet sites. News blogs, written by amateur journalists (citizens), which, although criticised for being more opinion than news, grab traffic – generally consisting of people who share the same opinions – have become very popular. These blogs can attract a huge number of visitors and become the primary news source for many people. Blogging and other forms of internet journalism have increased news content beyond anything previously imagined possible. Blogs are not just for amateur journalists. Mainstream media owners, realising the potential of blogging, have jumped on the bandwagon and encouraged their own journalists to get in on the act.

'Websites, podcasts, mobile phones and e-editions allow people to access news and entertainment on the move, whilst blogging enables readers to get directly involved with their newspaper. Video streaming and online television services are used by an increasing number of publishers, to provide news, sport and local information. These platforms are proving increasingly popular with regional press consumers.'

Newspaper Society

And new technologies have spilt over to broadcast news programmes, where viewers are invited to email or text their opinions on topical items. It is also now not uncommon for viewers to have their photographs and videos of news events broadcast on television – and get paid for it. The July 7 bombings in central London that killed 53 commuters in 2005 brought about a sea-change in journalism as the initial story was covered by mobile-phone photographers, text-messagers and bloggers.

Young people spend many more hours on the internet than watching TV, so broadcasters have had to devise strategies to capture this audience. The BBC is investing £300 million to develop online news services (subject to BBC Trust approval). Channel 4 plans to target a youth audience by setting up partnerships with social networking sites, such as Bebo, to provide online news. Other media companies are also trying to attract a youth audience this way. For example, the *Financial Times* has launched a Facebook application to give students free access to ft.com. To make all this information even more easily accessible, you can access latest news via RSS feeds straight to your web page/email.

Of course, traditional print newspapers haven't been the only media to be affected by the advent of the internet: the magazine sector has been hit too. While consumer magazines are prospering, other magazines have been adversely affected, despite the fact that, for many readers, the online edition of a magazine acts as a supplement or complement to the print edition. For some, there's no substitute for curling up on the sofa with a good old mag!

While there is growing concern over the future of print journalism in the UK, the situation in the USA is even more worrying. Circulation of most American newspapers has dropped dramatically. The *San Francisco Chronicle* is down nearly 30%. Cut-backs on big papers, including the national *USA Today*, have meant that confidence amongst journalists is not high and jobs are vulnerable. Added to this, it's the citizen journalists – the bloggers – who have recently broken many big political stories, including the controversy surrounding the resignation of Senate Republican Leader, Trent Lott. Talking about American journalism may seem irrelevant, but journalists must adopt a global perspective and that means watching developments in American journalism as they will surely follow in the UK. The 21st century has already seen changes in the industry and, as the nature of journalism constantly evolves and throws up more opportunities, the skills required to meet new challenges must also be acquired.

SEEKING THE TRUTH

We all hear of how journalists must be enthusiastic and persistent, have good spelling and accurate grammar, but we seldom hear mention of the need to be brave. In order to search out the truth, often in very difficult and complex situations, it is necessary to demonstrate the utmost courage. Part of our job as journalists is to feed the general public with the facts as we find them. War reporters put their lives at risk when they do this. Reuters' full-time journalist, Namir Noor Eldeen, and his driver, Saeed Chmagh, were tragically killed, in what was apparently a US helicopter attack, while trying to cover the conflict in Iraq. According to Reporters Without Borders, the number of journalists killed in the last five years has risen by a staggering 244%, with at least 86 journalists killed around the world in 2007 alone – more than half of these reporters died in Iraq. The total number of journalists killed covering the war in Iraq since it began has risen to 241. Four of these were British. Only three news organisations, the BBC, *The Times* and Reuters, have maintained their presence in Iraq since 2003.

HOW DO I GET IN?

Breaking into journalism, one of the most sought-after careers for graduates, is extremely competitive, and a first degree or equivalent qualification is almost compulsory. But that's not all: you need experience too. Targetting local print and online newspapers, local radio and trade or business magazines and ezines is more likely to get you work than the BBC or *Vogue* magazine. That's not to say you shouldn't try, but you stand a better chance targeting smaller publications and being realistic about your options. Chapter 5 gives you some ideas of how to go about finding your first job in journalism, and you can find information on work experience in Chapter 7.

When you do eventually break into journalism, probably as a general reporter or assistant press photographer, don't expect the salary to be earth-shattering, even if your writing is! Journalists, particularly at entry level, are not well paid. Chapter 4 gives you the low-down on salaries.

The decline in circulation of many print newspaper and magazines has meant that print media – while there is, of course, still a place for it, has become more vulnerable. However, journalists with online skills are working within a field that has opened up many possibilities. Consumer magazines produced for big companies, such as PC World and the Prudential, have seen huge growth. But it is important to note that a lot of the editorial (copy) is now outsourced – provided by freelance journalists. Freelancers tend to be journalists with plenty of experience and a good reputation. They might choose freelance work as an alternative to working in an office (with the managerial responsibilities of an editor or section editor which can go with that) because of the flexibility it provides – but it is not an easy field to get into unless you are already well established. You will find some top tips for freelancers in Chapter 2

LOCATION, LOCATION, LOCATION

While the internet has allowed journalists to do their work without ever having to enter a newsroom, the South East, particularly London, is still predominantly the base for most journalists. London is also where the national newspapers, television companies and most magazines are based.

This concentration of journalists in one area makes it harder for other regions to sustain their local talent and to provide opportunities for gifted individuals. The cost of living is also higher in the capital.

TRAINING

Journalists generally enter the industry by one of two routes: pre-entry or direct entry. The pre-entry method requires the journalist to take a vocational postgraduate qualification in journalism while the direct entry route means that the journalist finds a placement as a trainee. Both routes require prior work experience and generally a first degree. In exceptional circumstances, particularly if you are a mature person, you might get a place if you are able to demonstrate both a talent and a commitment to the industry, even if you are not a graduate.

A survey, entitled *Journalists at Work*, conducted by Skillset found that there was a definite need for skills development amongst journalists, particularly new entrants. Skill gaps included a lack of technological skills, especially the ability to work and write online. Employers reported selecting staff because they had these additional skills. Other problem areas were applicants' poor standard of English, inability to do shorthand and lack of knowledge of media law. Have a look at Chapter 6 for information about training.

HOW MUCH WILL IT COST?

Another problem that faces wannabe journalists is the cost of training. Mandatory grants are not available for postgraduate qualifications and discretionary grants are unlikely, although some organisations do offer bursaries to students who meet the necessary criteria.

'People "pay to enter", either via postgraduate courses or by working on unpaid work placements. The term, "the Samantha Syndrome" has been coined (by Professor Brian Winston at the University of Westminster) to describe the tendency of journalism to be increasingly middle and upper class in composition. The need to have wealthy parents to fund courses, or the willingness to face considerable debt, may be deterring potentially good students from entering journalism.'

Journalists at Work, Skillset/Publishing NTO, 2002

ROVING REPORTERS

Journalists often move across a number of sectors, from print and online to broadcast, or from radio to television, and so on. Working as a reporter for a news agency can provide opportunities for a journalist to work in all media as news agencies are the wholesalers of news to whoever wants to buy it. Working for different sectors requires learning different skills and in some cases, such as working in television, the journalist is required to multi-skill. You not only research, interview and write your report, but you may be involved in recording and editing it as well.

WHAT IS THE FUTURE OF JOURNALISM?

As for the future of journalism, no one really knows what that's going to be, but one thing is for sure, as a prospective journalist, you are going to need to acquire the technical skills to write online or in other digital media. The good thing is that online journalists who have the additional skills the internet requires can often expect better pay and feel less threatened by job cuts and redundancies.

Interview With Colin Meek

Freelance journalist, researcher, training provider and consultant

Colin Meek is a freelance journalist and has also trained journalists in techniques in advanced online research since 2005 . He has worked on many investigative projects for several publications on health and consumer affairs issues. Colin went freelance in 1997 after working as a principal researcher at Which?. *He was founding editor of the online news channel on journalism.co.uk called dotjournalism.*

How has the profession of journalism changed in the last five years with regard to new media?
On the one hand, there are new pressures and new challenges. Some journalists have suffered because their employers have demanded that they learn new skills and take on new responsibilities with little, if any, additional pay. On the other hand, where employers have been more progressive and flexible, journalists have been able to use new technology to enhance their roles.

How have new media affected print and broadcast journalism?
Six years ago the web was seen as a marketing tool for 'traditional journalism'. Now, it is generally accepted that the web is the dominant source of news for most people. But even more importantly, people are sourcing their news in radically different ways. For example, people turn to social networks and blogs for 'crowd-sourced' news. These trends are having a dramatic impact on traditional outlets and only the most dynamic and the most tenacious news teams will survive. While the freelance market is as competitive as ever, there are great opportunities for those who can grasp the new technologies and learn new ways of reporting.

What is the future for journalism?
The future of journalism is through telling stories in compelling, interactive ways. The best examples are in the Investigative Reporters and Editors archives. Journalists who contribute stories that allow the audience to interact with data and maps for example. Other stories that carry webcasts and podcasts. Stories that are updated through RSS feeds and allow readers to contribute comments and take part in online debates.

There is still a place for print journalism but that market will become dominated by a few authoritative broadsheets and some niche regional publications. On the whole the overall circulation figures continue to nosedive. Newspaper sites that simply carry the print version content will struggle. The best and most popular news sites are those that combine that content with web-specific content – the *Guardian,* for example. The magazine market will continue to flourish – especially those that commit to a strong online presence like *New Scientist.*

We will also see a rise in niche online publications and the scope for serious journalism here is tremendous.

What advice would you give to a would-be journalist?
Drown yourself in the technology of new journalism – HTML, CSS, blogging, interactive strategies, mapping and webcasting, among others.

NEW JOURNALISM DEFINITIONS

- **Citizen journalism** (aka participatory or public journalism) is a form of amateur journalism involving members of the public collecting, reporting, forming opinions of and disseminating news and information
- **Network journalism** involves a group of people working together on a single story via the internet
- **Participatory journalism** professional and amateur journalists working together
- **Open source journalism** collaborative work, similar to network journalism, but on material already published which is added to, or refined, and then republished.

CHAPTER 2

The jobs section

'With the explosion of multi-media publishing has come a whole assortment of new jobs.'

PPA

JARGON BUSTERS

- **ABC** Audit Bureau of Circulation: provides information on media-brands' cross-platform circulation and online traffic data
- **APA** Association of Publishing Agencies
- **Circulation** the number of print media distributed or sold
- **Consumer magazines** titles aimed at the general public on a wide variety of themes from interiors to music
- **Customer magazines** titles, with the appearance of glossy magazines, published by companies or businesses, such as John Lewis or the Prudential, targeted at potential or existing customers
- **JPEG** Joint Photographic Expert Group: commonly used computer picture file format

- **Layout** page design and format
- **Masthead** front page logo of a publication; or the publisher staff and contact details
- **Moblogging** images or text sent to a blog from a mobile phone
- **Pitch** presentation of a story idea to the commissioning editor
- **PPA** formerly known as the Periodical Publishers' Association
- **Skype** social networking software for making free calls over the internet to other users via a webcam (so allowing callers to see each other)
- **HTML** hyper text mark-up language: programming code for designing and displaying web pages
- **Tagging** descriptive labels attached to keywords on websites to make content more searchable.

Journalists work in all areas of the media – print, broadcast, online and new – and there are a multitude of different job titles, including reporters, bloggers, photojournalists, feature writers, fashion writers, editorial assistants, features assistants, political correspondents, film critics, presenters, broadcast journalists, sports commentators, science writers and all types of editors (fashion, arts, sports, etc).

It doesn't have to take that long to achieve your career goals, providing you have the talent, personality and tenacity to succeed. But if you *are* determined to become the next Trevor McDonald, Nina Nanah or Piers Morgan, you will have to begin somewhere – and that generally means right at the start as a trainee.

While many journalists find out about their first jobs through job ads, a lot get their first work by some other means, such as speculative letters, being in the right place at the right time, or being passed information by a person they know. This demonstrates that while looking for work you must check relevant publications and websites for situations vacant, and network. You need to put yourself out there, put your CV online and let everyone know you're available.

Publishers' contact details can be found in their publications themselves or you can look in the *Writers' and Artists' Yearbook*, *Willing's Press Guide* or *Benn's Media Directory*.

WHAT DO JOURNALISTS DO?

Journalists research, write and present news stories, features, views and reviews. This involves following up story leads (from the emergency services or general public), or generating your own, by interviewing relevant people by phone, email or face-to-face, even via skypecast. Interviews can be taped, noted down in shorthand or recorded for broadcast. Newspaper journalists may also work with a press photographer who will provide images to illustrate the news item or feature.

The news item or feature must not only entice the reader and be well written and easily understood, but must also reflect the house style of the newspaper, magazine, programme, website or other media for which it is written.

A lot of time can be spent working at your desk as well as being out and about investigating stories, interviewing people and attending press conferences or trade shows. This may involve travelling around the country or abroad and spending periods away from home. A journalist who reports on a particular region or topic is known as a correspondent.

ONLINE JOURNALIST

The internet has completely revolutionised the way journalists work. It can be used as a research aid, an archive and a way of connecting, both to interview sources and your audience. It also means that as a journalist, you no longer need to write from a newsroom.

Writing for the web still requires good journalistic writing skills, with added creativity. You must be able to tailor your writing style to the medium you are writing for, which also requires visual literacy, so the combination of imagination and planning are paramount.

The language style may need to be different when writing for the internet and your text needs to be broken up – longer, continuous pieces are unlikely to be read. Research has shown that the optimum reading line length is around 10 to 12 words – lines with more words than that tend to take longer to digest when read on the web. In fact, reading on a screen takes about 25% longer than reading hard copy. So, online journalists need to use shorter sentences and break up the text, keeping the actual article length much shorter than it would be in traditional print. The piece can also include click-links to other pages for further, more in-depth detail.

Remember that websites may be many pages long, with links leading from one page to another or to a completely different website. This is very different to the linear nature of print. Online journalists need to be very clear about what they are saying and information should be organised into sections, otherwise readers become confused. Online journalists can easily receive feedback or comments about their articles, which makes for a dialogue between journalist and audience.

EDITOR/NEWS PRODUCER

The editor (or news producer) is responsible for content – what appears in the paper, on the programme or on the website – and for identifying the target market. The editor manages the journalists with whom she or he consults regularly. Areas discussed include what news, topics or features to cover, which direction they should be taken in and how the final bulletin or feature should be edited. As well as delegating assignments, the editor may also conduct interviews and write news reports or articles. In broadcasting, the editor may also work on current affairs programmes, which might involve researching, producing and sometimes even presenting programmes too.

SUB-EDITOR

The sub-editor is responsible for preparing news stories or features for the press: thinking up headlines and sub-headings; ensuring language fits with house style; checking spelling and grammar are correct; and making sure content is accurate. The sub-editor must fit the story to the required length and make sure it reads well. In broadcasting, sub-editors may edit news items. Online sub-editing requires different technical skills (e.g. knowledge of HTML coding) and is more demanding than for print media, for instance it can include tagging articles with keywords.

NEWS EDITOR

The news editor has complete autonomy over the press or station's news or current affairs output, and must keep within an approved budget. This also involves having a dialogue with news organisations, locally, nationally and globally, and deciding which stories to cover, which journalist or reporter and film crew will cover it and the amount of time to be allocated on each story. When the reports have been prepared, the news editor must ensure their accuracy (in terms of both content and grammar), that they give a balanced view and that no laws have been contravened. In broadcasting, the news editor may occasionally also read the news.

This job description can also be applied to areas of specialist editing, for example a fashion editor on a magazine will be solely responsible for the fashion content of a magazine and the sports editor will carry overall responsibility for all sport-related content.

NEWSPAPERS

Newspaper journalists write about news and current affairs, covering politics, war, the economy, crime, natural disasters, health, business, sport, the arts and science. They work to extremely tight deadlines, having to turn around a story within a matter of days, hours or sometimes minutes, depending on whether the newspaper is a daily, evening or weekly. There is less time to conduct research and it is important that the journalist has a good list of contacts. Regional journalists live and work locally and personal involvement can lead to exclusive stories. Working online also requires additional technological skills – also featured in this chapter.

FASCINATING FACTS

British people are among the most avid newspaper readers in the world – 83.9% of all British adults (41 million people) read a regional newspaper, compared with 65% who read a national newspaper.

Newspaper Society

This fast-moving, adrenaline-driven pace adds to the excitement of life as a journalist, coupled with the fact that each day is different.

You are reporting on a political scam one day, and on a victim of mugging the next. Working in newspapers is more hard graft than glamour. You will have your scoops, but there is also the more mediocre, routine news.

> **FASCINATING FACTS**
>
> **'The regional press is a £4 billion industry with advertising contributing 73% of all revenues . . . Nearly 50,000 people work in the regional press; more than a quarter of these are editorial staff.'**
>
> **Newspaper Society**

FIRST JOB

Your first job will probably be on a local paper or website as a general news reporter or blogger – covering anything from local council meetings about uneven pavements to five-year-old Dylan Middlemore who is always sticking objects up his nose – before moving on to a more specialist area such as crime, sport, finance or arts and entertainment. As a specialist you will write news articles and more in-depth features.

When the news item or feature is complete, the sub-editor and editor will need to look at the copy (the text) to ensure it is suitable to print or publish online. The editor has complete autonomy and will make the final decision on what is to appear in the newspaper.

Some journalists work for news agencies, such as Reuters and Associated Press, rather than for a specific newspaper or website. The role of an agency is to sell the news and features that their journalists produce, to newspapers, radio, television and the internet – or wherever the news is needed. The news can be of regional, national or international interest, or specialist, such as that provided by Hayters Teamwork, the UK's leading sports reporting agency.

Laura Barnett
Commissioning editor, arts, the *Guardian*

I always knew I wanted to make writing my career – and as going straight into writing novels (my ultimate goal, like almost every features journalist!) seemed precarious and also a bit ill-advised for someone straight out of university, with a very narrow experience of life, journalism seemed the perfect way to do so. I did the postgraduate diploma in newspaper journalism at City University.

During pretty much every school and university holiday from the age of 16 I did work experience – and was still expected to do so when doing my postgrad course at City. Places I worked include Radio 1, *The Sunday Times*, *Bliss* magazine, the *New Statesman*, the *Independent*, the *Telegraph*, the *Fulham Chronicle*, and the *Bristol Evening Post*. It's depressing at times, can be fantastic, but either way is completely necessary in order to demonstrate your commitment to the job and build up a cuttings file.

While I was doing my course at City, I started doing unpaid arts criticism (theatre, dance and music) for the *Morning Star*. I think this amused the arts editor at the *Telegraph* when I did two weeks' work experience there during the Christmas vacation of the course. I started pitching ideas to her, wrote some stuff, and offered to keep coming in one day a week during that term (unpaid). I did that until Easter, then she asked me to stay on for four days a week (paid, but without a contract). So I became part of the arts desk from then on. Nine months later, after a three-month stint as junior commissioning editor on the *Telegraph*'s books desk, I applied for this job further to an advert in *Media Guardian* and got it. I've been here a year now. I write, commission and edit features for the arts section of G2. I get to work for the newspaper I have always read and contribute to an organisation of whose values I am truly proud. But I don't get to write as much as I would like.

The difference with online journalism (compared to traditional) means you have less time to turn it around and have to be prepared to enter into the fray of blogging – you have a much more direct relationship with readers.

I belong to the National Union of Journalists (NUJ) – absolutely vital to be a member, especially in these changing times. The chapel here at the *Guardian* is very strong – 97% of journos are members.

Advice?
Just make it happen. There's no point sitting around waiting for people to offer you a job or commission you – you need to get out there, make contacts, and offer things to people. I truly believe that if you're good enough and want it enough then you can make it happen, no matter what your background is or which university you went to. But do also consider doing one of the respected postgrad courses, as skills like shorthand – which very few people still learn – can make a difference in terms of how seriously editors take you.

When pitching freelance articles, do take the trouble to find out who the person is you're pitching to – and whether the thing you're pitching has already been covered. It looks *so* bad if you're pitching something that the same newspaper covered the week before – it looks like you don't really read it or understand what the paper does.

MAGAZINES

The magazine industry has of course been affected by new media. Many titles have seen a drop in circulation. According to the ABC,

FASCINATING FACTS

'The average UK adult now purchases as many as 30 magazines a year.'

PPA

from February 2008 all categories of consumer magazines, with the exception of soap magazines, have included titles taking a downward turn in their year-on-year circulation figures. However, on a more positive note, consumer magazine categories which also contain a considerable number of titles showing an improvement in year-on-year circulation figures include women's, men's, teens' and home interest.

FASCINATING FACTS

'The customer publishing industry is now worth over £680 million with a turnover topping £352 million.'

APA

The PPA reports that the diverse consumer magazine and business media industry is worth over £7.5 billion, the consumer magazine industry being valued at almost £3 billion. Out of all the magazines published in 2006 in the UK, 60% were business titles (5,113 titles). The market for customer magazines, such as those published by John Lewis or Tesco, is also very successful, attracting new clients and developing into digital formats. It is the second fastest-growing medium after online publications.

According to the PPA, the consumer publishing sector is projected to be worth £10 billion by 2010.

There are over 8,500 magazine titles published in the UK, 60% of which are business and trade magazines. Although customer magazines are an area of growth in the magazine sector, most would-be journalists want to work in consumer or lifestyle titles. In 2006, the number of consumer titles, or glossy mags, accounted for 3,445 titles, but, unfortunately, they are very difficult to break into. It is interesting to note, however, that 33 customer magazines appear in the top 100 by circulation and eight in the top 10. So, while this might not be the sector of magazine publishing you want to get into, if you do, you could be working on a magazine with a very high circulation, which would be great for your CV.

Magazines, print and online, unlike newspapers, are less concerned with current affairs and breaking news and more with feature writing. The turnaround time for magazines is generally longer than for newspapers, so the pressure is not so intense, and there is more time for research. Even so, magazine journalists still have to work to tight deadlines.

A magazine journalist has to generate, research and write feature articles that reflect the style of the magazine or ezine and meet the interests of the reader profile. Time is also spent at editorial meetings, where decisions on what to include in the next issue are made.

Magazine material is frequently outsourced, with much of the copy being produced by freelance writers. It is important for the freelancer to build up contacts and develop good working relationships with staff and editors, as he or she tends to work for a variety of magazines.

The magazine journalist can come up with ideas that will be put before the editor for approval, or be given work by the commissioning editor. Work will involve interviewing people, attending seminars, conferences and trade fairs. Working as a journalist for a magazine can also mean travelling round the country or abroad to do your research or get the interview you need. This can mean periods of time spent away from home.

Entry-level jobs in magazines are generally as junior reporter, staff writer, sub-editor, editorial assistant or production assistant. Many magazine journalists start out working for a trade or customer magazine, which, as mentioned above, may not be in an area they are interested in, but which provides a good way of learning skills.

Climbing the career ladder in magazines can be achieved surprisingly quickly. It is not unusual for editors to have only a few years' journalistic experience. Of course, this is determined by your talent and personality, as well as your tenacity.

Judith Wilson
Freelance journalist

I have always loved writing, and have been a consumer of magazines since about the age of 10! I originally went into book publishing as a sub-editor, but journalism appealed much more because I was interested in generating and writing my own pieces, rather than editing someone else's work. Also, I liked the quicker turnaround than book publishing. I love finding out about new products and trends, which of course is vital if working on a magazine.

I didn't train in journalism as such. I did a BA in English Literature at Leicester University, then an MA in English at Warwick University. Once I had joined a magazine, I basically learned on the job.

I started off as an editorial secretary for a scientific academic book publishing company, then moved to another similar company (Blackwell Scientific) – I started off sub-editing nursing texts, then was promoted to commissioning editor for nursing. I then went to Pavilion Books (illustrated coffee table books) as an editor. I left to be a freelance fiction 'reader' for publishing companies such as Penguin and Hodder and Stoughton. Then I got a job as a home writer on a general women's magazine called *Living* (not *Living etc, Living* is now no more!). I stayed there for two years, at IPC, mainly writing interiors features but also started to do some styling for shoots. Then went on to *Homes and Gardens* (also IPC) where I was Deputy Decorating Editor for three years, writing and styling big shoots. I left to go freelance in 1997, and still am. I have written on interiors for all the main magazines including *Saturday Times* magazine, *Saturday Independent* magazine, *Evening Standard, House and Garden* (I am contributing editor there), *Homes and Gardens, Living etc, BBC Homes and Antiques* etc, etc. I have also published 11 books on design – which I have written and styled.

I am still freelance, doing a mix of magazine journalism and also writing my 12th interiors book on *The Vintage Home*. I also lecture on styling at the KLC school of design.

Being employed by a magazine is quite different to being freelance – and I would recommend that everyone should do this first before attempting to go freelance. Working on a magazine is great fun – everyone cares a lot about the final product, there's a lot of team work, all the PRs, photographers etc are coming to see you so you are very up to date on trends. I loved it when I was on a magazine, but now I am freelance I love that even more! I like the variety, the fact that I am a specialist in my field, that I can combine doing books with articles, maybe a radio interview with lecturing, and so on. I don't do styling now – been there, done that! I prefer writing. I like the freedom that I have, although I make sure that I rent a desk space in an office so that I still get a sense of camaraderie.

Pros of my job – the satisfaction of writing, which I love, the pleasure of seeing the finished feature or book, going to press shows and being kept up to date with new stuff, the freedom of writing my own columns, which means I get to choose what I put on the page. Cons – only very occasionally worrying about the money side (it's not always particularly well paid) but generally I have plenty of work. Can't think of any other cons – I love what I do!

I belong to Women in Journalism, though rarely go to the functions, and am also a member of the Society of Authors, which has an informative quarterly magazine and also a free contract advice service.

Advice?
Go and do work experience on as many magazines as will have you! Speak up, get involved, offer to do writing, even if it isn't paid. As soon as you have a few pieces under your belt with a byline, it is your passport to greater things! Know your market – i.e. if you want to work at the high end of glossy

magazines, know what sort of journalist they are looking for and know the product, i.e. the magazine, inside out. Don't be afraid to put together thoughts and proposals. I got my first interiors book commissioned after I put together a proposal, with tear sheets and a rudimentary synopsis, rang up the publishing director, and refused to tell her what the book was about until I got into the interview. They commissioned me and it has since gone on to sell over 100,000 worldwide. Be brave! Also, once you have got your foot on the ladder, remember to build up and keep massaging your PR contacts, as they are invaluable.

Don't assume that just because you have a degree that it makes you special. It's possible to be a great journalist/stylist without a degree – what matters is a sense of style, a way with words, a total love of magazines, and a willingness just to get the job done. Send in your copy on time. Learn to write to the correct word count. Be professional. Spell editors' names correctly if writing to them. And, if asking for work experience, write rather than call or email – and make sure that your letter is beautifully typed, with correct spelling, and the name of the person you want to see also correct. Don't write to the editor, and it's not always worth writing to personnel departments. It's better to get onto the magazine itself doing work experience, because many positions get filled internally.

BROADCAST

Broadcast journalists work in local or national radio and television. Nowadays it is very common for journalists to cross over from radio to television. Television journalism is a highly competitive career to get into, so local radio often provides the first entry into broadcasting. Freelance reporters are common.

As the news is broadcast several times a day, updates or new stories have to be researched under strict deadlines with very little preparation time. Although the national industry is mainly based in London, regional reporters are needed all over the UK and abroad.

In order for a news item or bulletin to be broadcast, the reporter must first follow a story lead, or generate one, and then write and present it on the programme. The presentation of the news item might involve interviewing one or more people and the piece may be transmitted live or be pre-recorded. It may be necessary for reporters to edit their own bulletins.

Television journalists report from the relevant location straight to camera and may also be expected to record the news items themselves. Prepared reports must first be approved by the programme's editor before going on air.

In television, you can be an off-screen journalist, which involves doing research, establishing contacts, preparing interviewees (by informing them of the likely questions) and preparing and producing reports and items ready for broadcast. The off-screen journalist edits recorded bulletins and may provide voice-overs.

The newsreader assists in putting together the news reports that will be read on air and must introduce and link the news items delivered by the other reporters. Timing is crucial and the delivery must be accurate and correctly pronounced.

As young people are more likely to spend considerable time on their computers than watching TV, even broadcasters have had to look at alternative strategies to reach a younger audience via new technologies, such as corresponding websites, blogs and podcasts.

Jane Dreaper
Radio producer, Social Affairs Unit, BBC News

I graduated from Cambridge with a degree in social and political science where I also worked on *Varsity* – the student journal – as a reporter. I knew I wanted to be a journalist so, in my final year, I wrote off to about 50 newspapers all over

the country, beginning my career working for the *Chester Chronicle*, a respected weekly. I spent the first four months in Newcastle where I trained in shorthand, law and local government, and getting stories to offer to the local papers. I spent 15 months on the *Chester Chronicle*, writing and subbing on anything from local Women's Institute meetings to murder and scandal. It gave me a good foundation and taught me the basics of journalism. I got told off once because I covered a 50th wedding anniversary and got a detail wrong. It taught me the importance of being accurate.

In 1992, still a trainee, I began working for the *Sunday Sun*, a big regional and 'quite tabloid' paper. It was very strong on investigative journalism and very visual – there were a lot of photos, so it taught me to think in very visual terms, which stood me in good stead for when I began to work in TV.

In 1994 I moved to the newsdesk on the *Journal*, a daily regional newspaper, as assistant head of content. I was only 24, leading a team of two dozen journalists, which gave me an insight into management. It was a very satisfying job, but extremely hard work, working six-day weeks, 12-hour days.

I then moved to radio, Metro FM radio, a Tyneside local commercial station. It was very good experience to get myself on air, but I didn't get any training other than practising reading news bulletins, taping them and listening back. When I felt comfortable and they felt comfortable I went on air. The great thing about radio compared with newspapers is you can get news on air within minutes, with TV it is still reasonably quick but you have to think about the visuals and running time.

Metro FM was a small radio station with a small news operation and I soon reached my limits. In 1996 I moved to local BBC Radio Newcastle as a broadcast journalist. I was essentially a news producer, helping to put together stories for the breakfast programme.

I moved to London in 1997 on a six-month attachment to the BBC radio newsroom. It involved writing news bulletins from the correspondent and agent wires, editing, writing cues into the clips, giving it to the newsreader, getting it on air, and making sure people played the right inserts at the right time. It needed tremendous organisation.

I then began to wish I was out on the story more so in September 2000 moved to newsgathering, where I worked largely with special correspondents to cover education and family stories for TV and radio. Newsgathering is fast and furious. I sometimes worked 11 days on the trot getting up at 4.30am and finishing about six or seven in the evening. The producers would often ring me at 10 or 11 at night . . . There is a tremendous buzz – you run on adrenaline.

In the summer of 2001, I took up a newly created post as radio producer for the Social Affairs Unit of BBC News. This is where most of the domestic specialist correspondents are based. It's a real powerhouse! The subjects covered include health, education, crime, science, environment and the arts. My role now involves initiating original and investigative journalism, making creative radio packages, liaising with editors on the key Radio 4 and 5 Live news programmes, and overseeing the training and development needs of those connected with radio throughout the Unit.

I also do a lot of 'field producing' when I work with a correspondent wherever the story might be – mixing packages on my laptop, gathering audio by crouching on the pavement outside the story (e.g. courtrooms or the latest venue of fire strike talks) and making sure that the correspondent gets on air (whether we're in Birmingham or Bulgaria). It can be cold and often hungry work – but always rewarding to deliver!

Advice?

The best way to learn journalism is through local outlets – if you make a mistake it's to a smaller audience. Knowing the audience is a big thing. Think about newspapers and broadcast – decide which you want to do. If you go for an interview you must know the paper or have listened to or watched the programme so you have a feel for what it's about. You can always call the circulation department and ask for back copies of a newspaper. You need to be a people person – treat them sensitively and respectfully and think about your audience. In your final year at university get experience on a real local paper in addition to college or university papers or radio stations. Finally, enjoy the job. Journalism is fantastic fun.

PHOTOGRAPHY

Photography is another very popular career choice. The images used in the media can be an extremely powerful way of communicating a message and their value should not be underestimated.

Photojournalists work for magazines or newspapers and their website versions, providing both the words and pictures for a news item or feature article. This entails the work of a general journalist as well as producing the right pictures to illustrate the news item or feature. Photojournalists generally start out as photographer's assistants and learn the craft on the job.

The photographer's assistant helps with the photo shoot, which involves transporting people and equipment to the location or studio. They must then set up the lights and camera, answer the phone, deal with problems that occur and provide refreshments. The photographer's assistant may also attend college part-time.

Press photographers take the photos that illustrate the news item or feature. A lot of time is spent waiting around for the celebrity or newsworthy person to arrive in order to get the photo needed. As the photo moment can be over very quickly, it requires a lot of technical skill and precision to ensure that the moment is captured and that the right expression is caught to serve as the perfect illustration to the text.

Photojournalists and press photographers may also provide images for photo libraries and photo blogs and websites: they are paid whenever their pictures are used.

The picture researcher's job is to find the picture to match the copy for a newspaper, magazine, television programme, internet, or whatever medium is being used. This will either involve using images that have already been created or commissioning new ones. A list of contacts will be built up, both national and international, so that the picture researcher knows exactly where to go to get whatever type of picture is needed, whether it be a celebrity with her bra falling off or a politician wagging his finger outside the Houses of Parliament.

When an image is sourced, the picture researcher must deal with the copyright owner to ensure that the image can be used and the rights bought. Images can be worth considerable sums of money, so their details must be recorded, including whether the picture was used or not.

Images can be obtained from a number of sources including picture libraries and agencies (sometimes online), photographers, collectors, government departments, press offices, art galleries and museums, and architectural and design companies.

If a picture needs to be commissioned, the picture researcher must negotiate the photographer's fees, arrange the shoot, book the models and/or organise the props as well as arrange the location or studio.

Katherine Batchelor

***Press Gazette* student photographer of the year and *The Times*/Tabasco young photographer of the year**

When I left school I didn't really know what I wanted to do, but I liked art so I took an art course. Photography was part of the course and I found that it was this part that I was enjoying the most so I decided to pursue it. I then took a

photography and video course at Leeds College of Art and Design, which led me on to do a photography degree at Teesside University. As part of the degree we had to work in the industry for five weeks and I went to work on the *Yorkshire Evening Press* in York where I went out on assignments with photographers and got my pictures in the paper. I carried on working with the *Yorkshire Evening Press* and continued helping them out and having my pictures in the paper.

I then went to Sheffield College to do a postgraduate course in press photography where I did a week's work experience with the *Daily Telegraph* and Reuters News Agency. The course covered all areas of press photography. We had exams in caption writing, law, and the technological aspects of the camera and we had to work in industry for 18 months and then go back and do written exams.

At the completion of this course I entered and won *The Times* competition. The prize was a six-month contract working as a press photographer on all areas of the paper and a trip to Louisiana organised by Tabasco, who sponsored the competition. I spent a week travelling to Lafayette and New Orleans taking pictures on the subjects of food, Tabasco and the writer James Lee Burke.

At *The Times*, I enjoyed being on the newsdesk most of all because you were given something new every day. I also worked on features and sports. I went to a Chelsea football match, which is the first time I'd ever been to a big match. The photographer let me use his camera and I managed to catch the second goal, which was good. On features, I followed the photographers around to see how they did their jobs – mainly portraits of actors and artists. It was good to see how they took photographs outside of the studio, but made it look like they were in the studio. So even if I wasn't taking any pictures I still learnt a lot.

You need to have lots of patience. If you are having to photograph something you don't really enjoy and you have to wait for hours on end in the cold, waiting for the moment, it can be really boring and sometimes you still don't get the picture you want and this can be very frustrating. You can also get a hard time from the picture editor if you don't get the picture. But having your work in the paper is just brilliant. My first picture in *The Times* was eight columns. Knowing it was mine gave me such a buzz.

Advice?

Just go for it. I never knew whether I could do it or not, but going through college helped me gain confidence. I didn't think I could do it but I wanted to . . . But getting feedback from the tutors and getting work experience really helps. It gives you the boost to carry on. I really believe you've got to make it happen. If you really want to do it then you can get it. At the end of the day, anyone can take photos, but you've got to make it happen.

FREELANCING

Sean McManus has written freelance for *Melody Maker*, *Marketing Week*, *Bridge Design and Engineering*, *Internet* magazine, *Business 2.0* magazine and many more. He is the founder of journalismcareers.com and the author of the site's ebook *Journalism Careers – your questions answered*. His website is at www.sean.co.uk.

10 top tips for successful freelancing from Sean McManus:

1. Set up a website – if you write in a niche subject area, particularly for business-to-business publications, it can help to attract commissions if you post your portfolio online.

2. Contact editors direct – few editors will come looking for you. You have to find them. For an immediate response to a time-sensitive pitch, call them.

3. Differentiate yourself – make sure you know why you're the best person to write the story you're pitching.

4. Be professional – agree fees, copyright and payment terms in advance. Invoice promptly.

5. Meet deadlines – an average article received on time is more useful to editors than a dazzling article that's late.

6. Specialise – develop an area of expertise to write about and build your reputation there.

7. Network at trade shows – find the innovators and thinkers who can tip you off about the next big thing. Meet the magazine editors too.

8. Learn additional skills – study photography so you can sell pictures with your articles. Learn website design so you can sell articles ready for online publication. Learn to sub-edit and proofread so your articles are of higher quality.

9. Read – study your target publications so you can understand their style and then mimic it. Read as widely as possible to inspire new story ideas.

10. Unite – join a journalism union or other support organisation to tap into expert advice and support if things go wrong.

Fiona Murray
Freelance journalist

I'm a freelance journalist and I come up with ideas for features, which I then try to sell to magazines, newspapers and websites. I talk to commissioning editors about my ideas and they say 'yes' or 'no'; sometimes they approach me and ask me to write pieces they've thought of. At the moment I write mainly about parenting, children and education.

I did a degree in politics at Edinburgh University, then a postgraduate diploma in journalism at City University in London.

Before I left school I did work experience (for free) on my local newspaper. In my last summer before university one of the journalists was very ill so the paper paid me to work there for the summer. At university I worked on the student magazine; at journalism college we did two stints of work experience. I did one at a company producing in-house company magazines. My second spell was on the *Glasgow Evening Times*. I mainly just shadowed reporters, but got to write the odd snippet and picture caption.

After leaving City University I became a trainee reporter on the *Birmingham Evening Mail*. I wrote to practically every evening paper in Britain and actually got very few interviews – there was a bit of a turndown in the newspaper industry at the time. Birmingham hired about 12 trainees; it was a great start because they owned several weekly papers around the Midlands, a broadsheet morning newspaper, tabloid evening paper and a Sunday paper. We spent three months on different titles during our training and learned loads.

After qualifying I was a general reporter then a feature writer on the *Evening Mail*; I then became Women's Editor on the *Evening Mail* before leaving to go to Yorkshire Television as a news journalist. After that I joined the documentaries department and worked as a researcher and producer/director. I left because as a family we needed to move to Manchester. Then, with children, I decided it was easier to work freelance and go back to print.

Interviewing techniques?
On initial approaches for interviews, friendly and humble gets you a lot further than hectoring and aggressive. Shorthand is invaluable (wish I'd kept mine up); relying on tape recorders is dodgy (if it breaks you've had it), but now commonplace. Think through what you need from the interview first and

make sure you frame questions in advance; but don't stick slavishly to them if the interviewee reveals more interesting information: 'That was just before I murdered my wife'; 'So, what was your next album called?' Re getting information, the internet is invaluable.

Advice?

Make sure you read the paper/watch the programme you are applying to and watch/read actively; thinking of constructive, insightful comments. Don't be afraid to ask 'Why did you lead with "a" rather than "b"?'. Don't be arrogant and heavily criticise the paper/programme or you'll be out on your ear. If you are applying for jobs in journalism and have never set foot in a newspaper office or TV studio (depending on your preference), forget it. It's hugely competitive and there are hundreds of young hopefuls who will work for nothing to get the experience. Make sure your CV is free from spelling mistakes – basic, but it will put a newspaper editor off if you are sloppy. Above all be keen, willing and enthusiastic.

My work is rarely dull; I spend all my time talking to people and asking them (sometimes intimate) questions, ideal for the terminally nosy; I still enjoy writing and get a thrill when I find just the right turn of phrase. At the sharper *Daily Mail* end this is not a job for the faint-hearted. They demand their pound of flesh and have a strong political agenda, which you will be expected to follow. Journalists are not well regarded, though the majority are upright citizens who write honestly and accurately. As a freelance you miss out on the social side of office life, but it is hugely flexible which fits in with family life.

WORKING CONDITIONS

As news is, on the whole, a 24-hour operation, journalists working in news must be prepared to work long and unsocial hours: nightshifts are likely whether you are a new entrant or at a more senior level. Magazine journalists must also be prepared to put extra time in as and when necessary, particularly as the deadline looms.

Photographers often have to spend a large amount of time, often at unsocial hours, waiting around for a photo opportunity to happen. This can involve standing in the cold and rain for hours at a time.

Most journalists will spend some time on location and being away from home, but it is possible to take career breaks and return to the industry, or to work freelance, part time and possibly even job share.

Because of the pressure of tight deadlines, stress can be a factor, as stories must be originated, researched and presented within a very short period of time.

RELATED OCCUPATIONS

- Books and journals
- Databases and directories
- Public relations
- Technical author
- Researcher
- Fashion, advertising or editorial photographer
- Design
- Production
- Sales and marketing.

CHAPTER 3

Front page news: prospects in journalism

'A recent membership survey conducted by the UK Association of Online Publishers (the interactive division of the PPA) found that 40% of the online publishing workforce is female, but men are still more likely to become senior managers and directors.'

UK AOP

JARGON BUSTERS

- **Adobe InDesign** widely used desktop publishing program
- **Advertorial** advertisements that look more like editorial pages (must be labelled 'advertising promotion')
- **B2B** business-to-business
- **Browser** software (such as Internet Explorer or Firefox) which enables users to view web pages

- **Centre spread** middle two pages of a print magazine
- **Coverline** magazine cover caption
- **Cover story** leading story publicised on front cover of a publication
- **CTP** computer to plate: printing production technique without using film
- **DPS** double page spread
- **Draft** initial version of article before editing
- **Ezine** electronic magazine
- **Flatplan** plan of running order of pages in a publication
- **Gutter** margin surrounding text pages or columns
- **Header** information heading at top of page
- **House style** publisher's own guide to grammar, spelling and presentation
- **MPEG** Moving Pictures Expert Group: digital video file format
- **PDF** portable document format: used by Adobe Acrobat
- **Plate** metal or plastic sheet of page image used in print production
- **Rich media** artwork formats which allow multimedia or interactive content e.g. Flash and Java
- **TIFF** tagged image file format: format for transferring images between different applications and computer platforms.

FASCINATING FACTS

I think it's certainly true that the internet has created more opportunities for content creators but the vast majority of advertised journalistic roles are still for print roles or print/web hybrid roles. By 'advertised' I mean paid-for adverts; the fact that an organisation is prepared to pay something in order to recruit is usually a reasonable indicator of how they run their business. There are many more 'writing' opportunities online, but many of those will either be very badly paid or will expect you to write for free. In such scenarios, you would not expect quality journalism.

That said, it's certainly true that the required skillsets for journalists these days are changing rapidly. Multimedia skills are a prerequisite for many roles, so that's probably the most profound effect online journalism has had on the job market.

John Thompson, Managing Director, Mousetrap Media Ltd

NEWSPAPERS

The ABC's figures for March 2008 showed, with the exception of the *Sun* and the *Observer*, a decline in national newspaper circulation year-on-year. While traditional print media are continuing in a lot of cases to decline, their electronic equivalents are continuing to shine. Guardian.co.uk recorded a staggering 19.7 million unique users in January 2008, up 23% as a year-on-year figure. The *Daily Mail* and the *Mail on Sunday* had 17.9 million monthly unique users in January, which shows a 164% improvement year-on-year. This growth for unique users was also seen on other national newspaper websites, such as *Times* Online, the *Sun* Online and telegraph.co.uk. Not all traffic to websites is from the UK with *The Times* reporting that a third of its users were international.

The knock-on effect of digital dominance has meant that media publishers, such as the Guardian News and Media, are seeking staff with new media skills, which means that senior print journalists are facing voluntary redundancy.

STARTING OFF

Your first job on a newspaper, whether it be the print or online version, is likely to be as a general reporter for a local or regional publication. After that you may choose to specialise in a certain area, such as finance, science or politics, or a geographical region, and you may set up a blog, where readers can respond to and comment on your writings and/or photos. Other career possibilities include sub-editing or section editing.

TOP JOBS

- Section editor
- Editor.

If you have specialist knowledge of another country, you could become a foreign correspondent. British trained journalists covering international affairs are always needed. You may also be interested in moving into another medium altogether, such as television or radio.

FASCINATING FACTS

There are 1,309 regional and local newspapers in the UK: 32 mornings (22 paid-for and 10 free); 78 evenings; 18 Sundays; 532 paid-for weeklies; and 648 free weekly newspapers.

Source: Newspaper Society database as at 1 October 2007

Competition for entry-level jobs on newspapers is fierce and most trainees start out on a local newspaper before progressing to regional or national publications.

Journalists, photojournalists and press photographers working in newspaper journalism may be employed by either a large newspaper group such as Guardian Media Group, or by a regional newspaper company such as Johnston Press. The Newspaper Society website has information on daily, Sunday, weekly paid-for and weekly free newspapers in the UK.

Vacancies may be advertised in the Monday edition of the *Guardian*, the *Press Gazette* and on the following websites: journalism.co.uk, Hold the Front Page, the Newspaper Society, mediaguardian.co.uk, Prospects and Mediamoves.

Nicola Baird
Deputy editor, *Earthmatters*

Even at primary school I wanted to be a writer. I remember making and selling home-made magazines to my mum and dad (for about 10p) from about the age of eight.

At Friends of the Earth the deputy editor of *Earthmatters* works closely with the editor to produce a themed magazine that helps spread the organisation's remit – inspiring solutions to environmental problems. After the contents are planned I will have around 10 pages to commission or write (including the two-page books spread). Once the copy has come in I will work closely with the editor subbing to house style, cutting copy to fit and making sure that there are enough empowering stories and shorts talking about environmental justice in a very reader-friendly way.

Most of my training has been done at publications. While at IPC Magazines I did in-house training covering writing, subbing, libel and defamation, printing etc. I did a typing course – incredibly helpful – and have done shorthand, though don't use it at all. I also have a politics BA from the University of York and an MSc in environmental management. For the past 10 years or so it has been essential to have a Master's if you plan a career in the third sector (charities, non-government organisations (NGO) etc).

In order to get unpaid work I spent a lot of my time at sixth-form college and university creating and editing magazines. That showed editors I was committed to journalism – I worked for around three weeks at the *Yorkshire Evening Press* (on the news desk) and did a short stint at *Cosmopolitan*.

I've always been more interested in feature writing and my career was given a serious boost when I was one of the 12 short-listed in the *Vogue* talent awards. That helped me get a real journalism job: until that point I'd been working in the production offices of the publisher Dorling Kindersley.

I made use of the horse-riding qualification I have and took a job on IPC's *Horse and Hound* magazine – a weekly with an 80,000 circulation. I was in charge of at least 16 pages an issue and worked on the news and did subbing, as well as commissioning and supervision of some features. However, there's a bit more to life than horses, so I took a two-year post with VSO (Voluntary Service Overseas) and went to work as a journalism trainer for a development education NGO in the Solomon Islands.

I love feature writing – it's always good getting a commission. And I've written a number of books. Part of my job at Friends of the Earth is to write in-house books. Be warned: book writing is not paid well, but you get a real kick looking at the end result on a bookshelf, or better still, in a library.

The NUJ is a great organisation, really helpful, and if you are freelance and going through a lean patch that press card reminds you that you are what you claim to be, a journalist. The Society of Authors is a fantastic support too, especially if you don't get an agent – a task most people find harder than getting published.

Advice?
Learn to type, have a selling point, get a degree, do a journalism course, use the spell checker, learn to sub/proofread on paper and Quark (as well as another DTP system), decide about your ethical stand (would you flog a story about yourself or a friend, and if so, why?) and if you're getting into features be sure to think laterally. Entering your work in competitions doesn't hurt either, however naff it sometimes feels.

PRESS AGENCIES

Journalists can also be employed by press or news agencies such as Reuters or the Press Association. Press agencies are independent organisations that provide publications with news bulletins, features or pictures on local, regional, national and international affairs. They may also undertake specific reporting assignments. Large numbers of news correspondents are employed by the press agency and distributed around the region or countries from which the press agency reports. The National Association of Press Agencies provides information on agencies working within the UK. Some agencies cover a specialist area, such as finance, sport or agriculture.

Working for a press agency can provide you with the opportunity to experience working for print, broadcast, the internet and other digital technologies.

Justine Trueman
UK personal finance correspondent, Reuters

I spend about half of my time editing the funds and personal finance sections of the reuters.co.uk website and the rest writing articles for the web and wire. Immediacy is very important on a wire service. Some wire services take less care with stories (because of the time factor), so complicated finance issues aren't explained as much as they would be in a paper or magazine.

I did a degree with a major in journalism and minor in Russian language at Queensland University in Australia. My course is quite well regarded in Australia, especially for print journalism. I have also done the Securities and Futures Authority certificate, which is the exam a lot of stockbrokers take and gives you good background on UK financial issues.

I did work experience at three different TV stations over the summers while I was at university. They were local TV stations in my hometown, Brisbane. We weren't paid any

expenses, but it was really good experience and also made me realise I didn't want to be in TV! The best part was asking senior journalists how they got where they were. I also did movie reviews for free for a local street rag and voluntary work for an environmental magazine.

My first job was on a Sunday newspaper, which I got because I knew someone. I started off just doing one day a week and built up to three days. I was mostly copy-taking at first – just typing stuff in like the weather report, plus I did a fishing report, speaking to anglers and tackle shops up and down the coast. When someone left I took over the children's pages and wrote children's book reviews and also started up a kids' club. Later on I started a local business section because at the time there was very little local content. Then Rupert Murdoch closed the paper down, so I moved to Sydney.

I decided to move into finance. My next job was on a trade publication for financial advisers, then I got a job at the *Sydney Morning Herald*, which is Australia's largest daily broadsheet (a bit like *The Times* or *Telegraph*). After two years I moved to the UK and worked on an emerging markets publication. Then I was deputy editor of a pensions mag and had a brief stint as a city writer at the *Telegraph*; joined the dot.com boom and worked for a financial website for three years. I have also freelanced for *Time* magazine and *New Woman* plus a bit of industry stuff.

Interview tips?
Most people want to talk. It boosts their ego and if you are polite and pleasant and also sound like you know what you are talking about most people are quite flattered to speak to journalists. Good contacts are your life-blood.

Advice?
I think it helps to specialise, especially in this country. If there is an area you have a lot of enthusiasm for, that will come across in your writing and make it better. Plus you will understand your readers more.

It helps to have the guts to do things others wouldn't. Like ask a famous person for an interview (when everyone else is too scared), or ring up a big newspaper or magazine and offer to do freelance work. The key to journalism, I think, is persistence – like chasing stories when everyone is being very elusive.

MAGAZINES

'A recent survey conducted by the UK Association of Online Publishers showed that 48% of respondents preferred their publication's website for ease of access. However, half of the respondents favoured print magazines as a more satisfying choice.'

PPA

Jobs in magazines include general staff writer, assistant editor, sub editor or section editor. Other possibilities include freelance work – working for a number of different publications or media, including online magazines or ezines.

TOP JOBS

- Editor
- Publisher.

Gilly Sinclair
Editor, *Woman's Weekly*

The job of editing is about ensuring that the content, editorial direction and positioning of the magazine serves its market in the best possible way. *Woman's Weekly* is one of the country's oldest magazines, it launched in 1911, and has an extremely loyal following. It's my job to delight existing readers each week whilst attracting new ones. We target mature, intelligent women who are interested in traditional skills and values. They want to celebrate their lives, their homes and their families.

I'm a newsagent's daughter so I grew up surrounded by newspapers, comics and magazines. Reading everything in my path became second nature. I was always going to be a journalist. I attended Harlow College for its year-long course in journalism, working at the *Havering Recorder* newspaper in college holidays.

After college I spent the first six years of my career on the *Havering Recorder* where I did a bit of everything, from feature writing, to crime and court reporting and later sub-editing. It was a fantastic way to learn the craft of a journalist. I also worked in public relations and then magazines, at *TV Times*, *Take a Break* and as a freelance sub-editor on a number of titles.

An editor today needs to be a good journalist, a good manager of people and a business person, too. It's important to feel excited by the job every day: every story, every person, every event. Editorial passion is a massive driver. When recruiting I look for job knowledge, a passion for the written word, a determination to be the best and a personality that will encourage and invite communication.

What makes a good journalist?
It's a tough one, this! But you know it when you meet it. It's a passion and zeal for both getting the story and writing it; a determination to tell a good story in the best possible way.

Advice?
I would encourage would-be journalists/editors to read everything, listen to everyone, observe minutely your surroundings and write all the time.

FASCINATING FACTS

The total value of the UK magazine industry is £7.2 billion. This can be broken down into 49% business media, 41% consumer and 10% customer magazines.

Source: PPA/APA, November 2007

In 2006, the total number of magazine titles were: 3,445 consumer; 5,113 business media; and 1,300 customer. Magazine titles have increased by 55% since the launch of the commercial internet.

Source: Advertiser's Association, November 2007

Magazines may be produced by large publishing groups producing numerous titles, such as EMAP Consumer Magazines or IPC Media, or by specialist publishers who produce in-house free or paid-for magazines, such as Haymarket, Reed Business Information and Cedar Communications. Added to this, many larger companies and charities employ journalists to produce their own in-house titles.

Consumer or lifestyle magazines, such as *Nuts* or *Cosmopolitan*, are the most popular and therefore a harder genre to break into. Consumer magazines are either targeted at a particular group of people – for example women (*Grazia*), or young teens (*Shout*) – or at a specialist interest such as *Amateur Gardening* or *Country Homes and Interiors*.

'75% of all UK adults and 84% of all 15–24-year-olds read a consumer title.'

NRS (National Readership Survey) 2007

Business, B2B, and customer magazines are where new entrants tend to start off. These magazines are not normally found on your newsagent's shelf, but BRAD (British Rate and Data) provides a comprehensive list of them, so check out their website. Business media are specialist publications targeted at the people working in an industry, for example *Farmers Weekly*, or aimed at people working in professional careers, for instance the *British Medical Journal*.

Customer magazines are published at least twice a year, either in-house or on behalf of an organisation, as a way of connecting and communicating with customers. A cross between consumer and business media magazines, the customer magazines are there to increase either sales, loyalty or satisfaction, and include titles such as the *National Trust Magazine* and Waitrose's *Food Magazine*.

Online magazines include historictraveler.com and *Ability Magazine*. Some ezines are small privately run websites, while others support brands already available in other media.

Job vacancies are advertised in Monday's edition of the *Guardian*, *Campaign* and *Media Week* (including their supporting websites). Job advertisements can also be found on the websites of publishing companies, such as EMAP Communications and IPC Media, as well as Prospects and a whole host of other websites such as PPA and journalism.co.uk.

Scott Manson
Editor, *Loaded*

As editor of *Loaded*, I oversee the creation and production of the magazine from the front cover to the back and I manage 22 staff. I have line managers who have clusters of people who report to them, but I am the overall manager.

It sounds a bit of a cliché, but I loved writing and I was really bad at maths – that side of my brain doesn't seem to work. I think I failed my maths O level about three times, so my word side was amped up to compensate for that. I got As in English and I did English at university, where I worked on local newspapers and magazines. I went into magazines for two reasons: 1) I didn't want to wear a suit; and 2) I wanted to get free CDs and to get into clubs and places on the guest list.

The English degree I did at Leeds was 20% vocational. You had to find six weeks' work placement in years one and two.

That more than any other part of the degree was what got me my first job. I was working for a magazine called *Venue*, and I got to write something after about three or four weeks. They liked what I wrote. I went back to work for them over the summer holidays. I was the country pubs reviewer. I had to visit two pubs every day and have a drink in the first one and another drink and a meal with a landlord in the second. I then had to go and write about it. I didn't get paid any money of course.

While I was at university, I was working for *Venue* and putting together festival supplements and I did more writing and editing, so I had built up a portfolio by the time I left in 1995. My first job was for a publishing contractors called Square One in Clapham who publish various magazines. I was made editor straightaway and worked on a free magazine with a circulation of one million called *All Days* magazine, which was distributed in the All Days shops (a chain of convenience stores) nationwide.

Working for a contract publishers is very good. I would really recommend it to anyone interested in going into journalism. It's a very good discipline because you have to write about stuff that you don't like and are not interested in, like cat food bought by old ladies. It teaches you tone and discipline. I got to do picture research as well and you can end up designing the whole thing yourself.

What makes a good journalist?
An ability to turn things on their head, an ability to turn things round quickly and to be able to put a twist on every feature they do. It's also important to have the ability to take criticism. You also need to have the ability to get out there and do something. Don't just do your research on the internet. You must talk to people and meet them face to face.

Advice?
Make sure you read the magazine. Make sure your ideas are original. Don't write a letter and say I can make the coffee

and I don't mind filing. That just makes you sound stupid. I can't tell you how many letters we receive like that. It is best to say, I loved the last issue, these are three things that I liked, this is what I would have done differently and here are three new ideas. Also what is really difficult for me is finding people who are funny. One skill worth learning is how to write a genuine article which is amusing.

BROADCAST

Broadcast journalists generally enter the profession working in the newsroom before becoming a reporter. They may work for news or current affairs programmes, writing and researching news bulletins or reports. Some broadcast journalists move into presenting their own reports as well as becoming correspondents on a particular subject, such as finance or politics, or for a particular region or country, but this area is more competitive to get into.

Broadcast journalists are increasingly required to both present and record their own reports, which means developing technical and administrative skills. Working for both radio and television is common, with organisations such as the BBC often requiring you to do both. Broadcast channels will also have an online equivalent, with a web page within the website for each programme broadcast. Broadcast journalists may also provide blogs or podcasts for these sites.

Broadcast journalists may also move across to other media including online news or work on documentary programmes as researcher and presenters.

TOP JOBS

- Presenter
- Newsreader
- News editor.

Employers include:

- The BBC (national and regional radio and television stations, freeview stations and the international World Service)
- ITN and regional ITV companies
- Channel 4 and S4C
- Independent national and local radio stations and production companies
- Satellite and cable television and radio
- International news agencies.

Vacancies are advertised in *Broadcast*, the Monday edition of the *Guardian*, the *Independent* and *Campaign*, as well as on the following websites: mediaguardian.co.uk; journalism.co.uk; BBC and other production company or station websites.

Contact details of employers can be found in the *Writers' and Artists' Yearbook* and the *Media Directory* as well as various websites such as journalism.co.uk, newspapersoc.org.uk and ppa.co.uk.

John Pullman

Programme Editor, ITN (formerly head of news and current affairs, Local Programmes Department, Granada Television)

Granada was generally bombarded with letters from journalists looking for work. As they came in we would sift through them and put the promising candidates to one side. Then when a job came up we'd call them in for interview. If anyone's letter stood out particularly I would bring them in for a chat, sometimes offer some freelance work to try them out, and then if I wanted them to stay, try to find a vacancy. It

was rare for us to advertise, but if the job was specific in terms of location or role then we might use an advert in the trade press – or local paper.

Everyone in an editorial role in the newsroom had to have a journalistic qualification. We never took on anyone straight from college. Everyone I hired as a journalist had had a previous job – usually in radio or newspapers. The best CVs showed evidence of serious journalism – not work in PR or marketing, which people sometimes try to disguise as useful experience. Newspaper cuttings are useful, a TV showreel even more so. Recommendations from previous bosses and colleagues were helpful too.

It's important for candidates to know about the TV programme/newspaper/radio station they want to work for. It was amazing the number of times people who applied for jobs hadn't seen the programme. It's unforgivable. You should get hold of tapes or back copies before you arrive for the interview – and make sure you know what's happening in the region. You need to know about a broad range of subjects – politics, sport, showbiz etc. Most journalists start out as general reporters – so you can't afford to have a blind spot.

It's also important that CVs are accurate. A CV with a spelling mistake goes straight in the bin. Work experience was useful in the sense that it showed a level of commitment to the job. Usual qualifications were either a degree, an NCTJ qualification or a diploma in journalism.

What makes a good journalist?
Journalists need to be tenacious, articulate, committed to the job, interested in the world, nosy by nature, and hard working. You're unlikely to make a good journalist if you're a lazy, clock-watching, shy, tongue-tied recluse who doesn't like meeting new people.

Advice?
Be persistent. Do your homework.

ONLINE

Newspapers, magazines and broadcast are no longer disconnected from the internet, but work with it to supplement and incorporate the dissemination of news. With young people spending more time on the net than watching TV, traditional media have had to utilise the advantages of digital technology to create a future that the younger generations of today can be part of and respond to. However, not all news sites or ezines on the web are connected to traditional media. Some ezines are only available as a website with no print equivalent. Finding work for one of these sites, however, is not dissimilar to finding work in traditional media. You should follow the advice in the newspapers, press agencies, magazines and broadcast sections above.

PICTURE RESEARCHERS

Employers include:

- Newspapers
- Magazines
- Television
- Multimedia
- Book publishers
- Internet publishing
- Art galleries and museums.

Vacancies are advertised in Monday's *Guardian*, the *Bookseller* and *Campaign*.

Bernie Menezes
Picture researcher, *Time Out*

I studied photography at polytechnic, because originally I wanted to be a photographer, as most picture researchers do, but it was far too competitive and cut-throat. I enjoyed taking pictures as a hobby and a friend of mine from the *Daily Mirror* suggested that I do picture research.

I started off at a picture agency, London Features International, where I was researching for clients who might be asking for pictures of celebrities or pictures of celebrities doing certain things. You really need to know about current affairs, film, television, all sorts of media – you have to keep in touch and read all the newspapers and magazines.

Most of what I do involves getting in the pictures for the listing sections and some of the main features. There are seven different sections to *Time Out* and there are three staff: the picture editor, the deputy picture editor and myself, and the work is divided up between us.

What makes a good picture researcher?
You have to be enthusiastic and keen. You are not very well paid at picture agencies, so you have to really want to work, and you do work very hard, especially at junior level. You need to be interested in media and related affairs. *Time Out* is a weekly magazine so the turnover has to be very quick. We have to provide pictures within an afternoon or an hour. Most agencies deal online now so we can download pictures within a couple of minutes. In the old days we would have had to search the library then order a bike and get the picture biked over so it took considerably longer. It's quicker now and less expensive, because you don't have to pay the search fee.

I enjoy working at *Time Out* very much, because it is about the things I am interested in: art, music, books and films. I enjoy the relaxed feeling of the office and everyone is quite friendly and we are all working towards something we enjoy seeing at the end.

Advice?
Be keen and build up a portfolio of photographs you like, look in magazines and take cuttings from the photographers you admire. Making a book will impress people, and so will work experience. You need to know about what's going on in film, television and so on.

Researchers starting out should also build themselves a book of contacts, which will prove invaluable especially if you're moving around to different desks as a freelancer. Contact books should have the following numbers:

- Photographers
- Stylists
- Make-up artists
- Studios for hire
- Model agencies
- Film PR and distributors
- Music PR
- Record companies
- Picture agencies
- PR companies
- Publishers
- Theatre PR

- Magazines and newspapers
- Entertainment venues
- TV channels
- Other freelance picture researchers
- Galleries and museums.

Freelancers who don't have their own contact books and spend most of their time pestering busy staff on the desk for numbers are not likely to be hired again.

Picture agencies are a good way to get your foot on the ladder to being a picture researcher or editor. You get to know the picture editors on publications who will always remember if you were particularly good or efficient at getting their requests done as well as picking up a good knowledge of photography in general.

Always keep up with current photographers, go to exhibitions and see as many portfolios as possible of established photographers and students or graduates.

CHAPTER 4

Salaries in journalism

'Recent surveys have shown that:

- Nearly half of all journalists earn less than the average wage in the UK. 75% of journalists earn less than the average wage of a professional worker.
- 80% can't afford the average house mortgage.
- Journalists' starting rates are at least £7,000 less than the median starting salary for graduates.

Yet surveys also show that pay in unionised workplaces is 8% higher than in non-unionised ones.'

NUJ

JARGON BUSTERS

- **Byline** journalist's name on an article
- **Commission** request to journalist by sections editor or editor to produce an article for a fee

- **Coverline** brief details, highlighted on cover, of magazine contents
- **Cuttings** journalist's published work contained in portfolio to show prospective employer
- **Disco donut** discussion with two or more guest speakers, usually coordinated from a TV studio, introduced and summarised by correspondent (source: NUJ)
- **Generic minute** first report from correspondent after a breaking story
- **NUJ** National Union of Journalists
- **Subheads** small headings used to break up an article.

FASCINATING FACTS

Incomes in journalism vary enormously with some freelancers who get very little work earning below £5,000 a year, to others who earn in excess of £100,000. The average income (gross full-time pay) for journalists and editors working on newspapers and periodical is £29,527 (median value) or £33,203 (mean value).

According to the National Statistics for 2007, 10% earn £17,999 or less; 20% earn £21,701 or less; 25% earn £22,813 or less; 30% earn £23,710 or less; 40% earn £26,066 or less; 40% earn £32,527 or less; 70% earn £35,999 or less; 75% earn £37,458 or less.

Source: National Statistics figures for 2007

The amount a journalist is paid depends on a variety of factors. The first is experience; the greater the experience the journalist has the more he or she is likely to be paid.

Rates paid for journalistic contribution also vary by sector, with those working in the more popular areas of national newspapers and television earning more than those working in regional and local equivalents. Online skills can also boost your income. An online sub-editor will generally earn more than a traditional sub-editor because more technical skills are required.

Journalists on permanent contracts earn, on average, more than those on temporary contracts because their work is consistent. Freelance journalists must negotiate their own rates with the commissioning editor, but these will vary considerably depending on the size of the company, the experience of the journalist and so on. Rates may be paid according to the word count, generally calculated per 1,000 words. If you are freelance you will have to pay your own tax and National Insurance, cover your expenses, holiday leave and pension schemes and pay for all your regular bills out of the money you make, so don't forget to take this into account when negotiating your rates.

Another factor is the commercial value that the editor places on the story or picture. A scoop about a politician's infidelity will pay better than a routine story about a golden wedding anniversary. But a commissioning editor may also pay the least amount possible by using less experienced journalists or even those on work experience. Some journalists on small publications may not even be paid at all.

Pay will also depend on the publisher. Larger companies, such as those that own national newspapers and websites, will obviously pay more than a small local free newspaper because national papers have larger markets and are more profitable.

According to the Journalists at Work survey, many journalists are satisfied with the level of their pay. Those who are dissatisfied tend to be new entrants. This, of course, will be you. Are you prepared to work in an industry that will not reward you financially with what you think you may deserve?

Below are examples of the minimum rates that the NUJ has provided for freelance journalists as a starting point for negotiation. Please note that rates do vary enormously in many cases and you could earn a lot more, but the figures below are the least you should expect as a freelancer.

BROADCAST

BBC AND NATIONAL TV

Broadcast is not the best paid area of media. Rates are highest for Group A (network TV) and least for Group D (local radio). Group F rates cover use of works on broadcasting websites.

- Group A: reporting (using BBC camera, crew and equipment): £236 per day
- Group D: reporting/production (for novices straight from college): £83 per day.

COMMERCIAL RADIO

Day rates from 2007–08, for college student or leaver within six months of completing course (including reporting) range from £74.71 to £120 for more experienced reporters.

PROGRAMME SUPPORT

Broadcasting organisations often produce info-packed factsheets and glossy publications and web material to support their programmes. Rates for this work are:

- Editing/sub-editing: £275 per 1,000 words
- Editing/sub-editing: £200 per day
- Writing or reporting: £285 per 1,000 words
- Writing or reporting: £180 per day.

ONLINE DIGITAL MEDIA

EDITING AND PRODUCTION

Rates vary widely.

- Sub-editing: £160 per day
- Sub-editing with HTML coding: £240 per day

If the sub-editing work includes markup it should attract a higher fee.

WRITING AND RESEARCH

Rates are for work commissioned for first publication online but be aware that rates and terms vary widely:

- Writing: £160 per day
- Writing with intense research or background: £350 per 1,000 words.

PHOTOGRAPHY

Again, rates vary widely.

NEWSPAPERS AND MAGAZINES

- Commissions for category A (large circulation glossy mag) photo, minimum day rate: £500
- Stock picture (half page for regional newspaper): £100.

BROADCASTING

Exclusive new pictures will command four-figure transmission fees, but even stock pictures could be worth a few hundred if used, repeated and broadcast in other territories.

STOCK PICTURES

- Single transmission (up to 4 seconds): £85
- Single transmission (up to 10 seconds): £110.

ONLINE USE OF PHOTOS

The NUJ recommends 'watermarking' photos online to help track unauthorised copying.

ADVERTORIAL AND NEWSPAPERS

- 600 × 800 pixels: £175 per month
- 600 × 800 pixels: £625 per year.

EDITORIAL

- 600 × 800 pixels: £130 per month
- 600 × 800 pixels: £425 per year.

PICTURE EDITING AND RESEARCH

- Broadcasting: £190 per day
- Magazines: £125 per day
- National newspapers: £130 per day.

PRINT MEDIA

MAGAZINES

Magazines Category A: large circulation and glossy mags

- Writing: £500 per 1,000 words
- Section or production editor: £230 per day.

Magazines Category D: smaller magazines

- Writing: £230 per 1,000 words
- Section or production editor: £145 per day
- Reporting or researching: £130 per day.

NATIONAL NEWSPAPERS

- Writing, reporting and researching page lead (tabloids): rarely less than £700

- Splashy features for 'qualities': from £600 per 1,000 words
- News for 'qualities': from £280 per 1,000 words.

REGIONAL NEWSPAPERS

- Writing, reporting and researching for regional daily (ordered story or feature, bigger pages): £150 per 1,000 words
- Writing, reporting and researching for local weekly (ordered news or feature): £100 per 1,000 words.

For further information on the recommended NUJ freelance rates for journalism, check out the NUJ Freelance Fees Guide at www.gn.apc.org/media/feesguide. You will also find plenty of useful tips regarding ways to negotiate your salary.

CHAPTER 5

Getting into journalism

'You must love to write and experience new things. Be prepared to network. Learn to accept criticism. Don't expect to earn a lot of money. Be prepared to work 24/7, this is not a 9–5 job. It's all about tenacity. Do not get frustrated and more importantly pitch, pitch, pitch. The more story ideas you come up with, the better chance you'll have of writing them.'

Dee McLaughlin, editor, Virgin Megastores' online magazine

Journalism is a tough industry to get into. It has a strong emphasis on qualifications and work experience, but these alone will not guarantee you work. You need to have certain personal attributes, skills and relevant knowledge.

PERSONAL ATTRIBUTES

Look at the lists below and see if you have what it takes to become a successful working journalist.

You must have:

- Creativity
- A passion for words
- Passion for journalism and/or a specialist subject
- Enthusiasm and persistence
- Good social skills
- Courage to get to the truth
- A keen interest in innovation and emerging technologies.

You must be able to:

- Work on own initiative as well as be part of a team
- Sniff out a good story
- Ask hard-hitting questions
- Understand complex issues and translate them in an uncomplicated, accessible way
- Make your writing interesting to read and easy to understand
- Conform to editorial policy
- Work well under pressure to tight deadlines, working long, irregular hours
- Accept criticism from the editor or reader.

You must be:

- A good communicator
- Determined and tenacious, focused and resilient

- Inquisitive and persistent
- Self-motivated
- A good listener
- Balanced and objective
- Well organised.

SKILLS

There are some skills that it is essential to have and others that are preferable or useful. Check the following lists to see if there are any areas you need to work on.

ESSENTIAL SKILLS

- Excellent grammar, perfect spelling and punctuation
- The ability to check that your work is factually accurate and the content legal
- The ability to communicate to a variety of audiences in a variety of media – to be able to express yourself whether with an individual writing style or a clear, authoritative broadcast voice
- IT skills: for example word processing, QuarkXPress, InDesign, online writing skills
- The ability to use email and the internet for both internet and hard copy publications and even text messaging
- Self-promotion skills – particularly important for freelancers.

PREFERABLE SKILLS

- An ability to type and use shorthand
- A driving licence.

OTHER USEFUL SKILLS

- Good basic knowledge in key areas, gleaned through personal experience and interests and relevant training
- An exceptionally keen interest and understanding of people, places and events
- Knowledge of and interest in current affairs at all levels
- Good knowledge of journalistic law.

QUALIFICATIONS

'It's certainly true that the required skillsets for journalists these days are changing rapidly. Multimedia skills are a prerequisite for many roles.'

John Thompson, Managing Director, Mousetrap Media

Journalists study a wide variety of degree courses, not necessarily related to journalism. Some employers may be of the opinion that this makes the applicant a more rounded person, or gives them specialist knowledge. Although the degree subject is, in many ways, less important than the qualification it gives you, studying politics, public administration or economics may improve your chances of work. Media studies may be frowned upon, so if this is the degree you wish to do, choose a well-respected course. There are, of course, an increasing number of well-regarded journalism degree courses available.

Even if you are a graduate with work experience and you get an editorial post, you will probably have to do a part-time postgraduate course, which can take anything from nine weeks to a year or more to complete.

In order to be accepted on a pre-entry course or as a direct entrant trainee you will need to complete an application form, do a test in

English, writing ability and general knowledge and complete an interview.

The only occasion where qualifications are likely to be less important is when talent, good contacts and plenty of work experience (demonstrated in your portfolio) are in evidence. This is more likely to apply to a more mature person.

BBC and ITN news trainee schemes require you to be highly qualified, talented and with a good portfolio of work experience. They are hugely competitive, and thousands apply for one traineeship.

See Chapter 6 for more information about training and courses.

WORK EXPERIENCE AND PORTFOLIO OF WORK

While qualifications are important, you stand little chance of getting paid work without having first done some unpaid work. In order to prove your commitment to the particular field of journalism that you wish to go into, you must have completed a considerable amount of work experience. This should culminate in a portfolio of cuttings and/or showreels for presentation to your prospective employer. It is not enough to have just worked on university newspapers or hospital radio; you must have done some work experience for a more respected publisher or broadcaster, for example a local newspaper, radio, website or trade or business magazine.

NEWSPAPERS

Working in newspapers is the most popular career choice for journalists. However, it is unlikely, as a new entrant, to get a job working for a national paper.

You will need to do a pre-entry vocational course or enter a newspaper company direct, where you will receive in-house training. You will probably need to have a degree with an impressive portfolio of work experience to demonstrate your commitment to journalism.

Mike Baess
Corporate journalist, Tesco

I always wanted to be a journalist and pestered my local paper, the *Camden Journal* in North London, into giving me a job. I was halfway through my A levels and it was a case of take a job now or go on with my education with no certainty of getting work.

After getting my job I was sent on two eight-week block-release NCTJ courses at Harlow Technical College in Essex. I was working for six months before I got sent on the course. I started off as a general reporter and one of my jobs was doing obituaries.

I went on to become the crime reporter and had to visit the police stations in Camden to find out who had been murdered and follow up the stories. I felt like I was living in some kind of Film Noir. There is no better way of learning the ropes than to work for at least a couple of years on a local paper in a great news area.

Interview techniques?
If your shorthand is not that good get the interviewee to repeat key information by getting them to elaborate. That gives you good time to get key points down. Train your ears to hear only the parts of an interview that will make the story. There's no point in taking down everything. This comes with time.

Advice?
In job interviews show keenness by asking questions. Don't sit back and just answer the interviewer's questions. Show you know about the job you're going for and make sure you have read the most recent issue of the magazine/paper. Keep CVs to no more than two pages.

MAGAZINES

Qualifications to degree level are increasingly required to get into magazine journalism. Many new entrants have gained pre-entry certificates accredited by the NCTJ (National Council for the Training of Journalists) or Periodical Training Council (PTC) or postgraduate courses in journalism.

Sadie Sheppard
Features editor, *Amateur Gardening*

I have to write at least two features per week (very short deadlines!), source pictures, commission other feature writers to write stuff, source pictures for them, interview people, go to press trips, location filming etc. I started as gardening writer, was promoted to features writer and promoted again to features editor.

I just always loved writing. I did a BA in communications at university – half English, the other half about journalism, publishing, editing etc.

I had all sorts of work experience: PR, marketing, press-release writing, website stuff etc. My first job was working in an art gallery, and part of that work was producing glossy brochures for sales. I got the job by responding to an ad in a paper.

Advice?
For interviews/CVs: sell yourself strongly – in this business, people seem to be looking for that kind of confidence even if you don't really feel it.

Don't sit too long in front of a blank page. Always start writing, anything, doesn't matter what it is. It can always be deleted later when the good stuff starts coming. And don't be too precious – don't be upset when editors alter what you've written – you are never bigger than the magazine.

BROADCAST

New entrants to broadcast journalism are generally in their mid-20s. If you are 40 or over, you will find it difficult to break into this highly competitive field of journalism, unless you already have an established career in print journalism.

In order to get into broadcast journalism you will need to have a first degree in a specialist subject such as politics, finance or the environment. You can then either take a vocational pre-entry course in broadcast journalism recognised by the National Council for the Training of Broadcast Journalists (NCTBJ) or enter directly on to a trainee scheme, such as those which are occasionally offered by the BBC or ITN (check out their websites or look in the *UK Press Gazette* for trainee opportunities).

Plenty of work experience is another entry requirement, as is a good knowledge of how the industry works at all levels.

Reporters who will be presenting on air should have a clear broadcast voice, should not gesticulate wildly (if on television) and should have visual flair. It is not that uncommon for things to go wrong on live news coverage, so the reporter or newsreader must have the ability to remain calm and think on his or her feet. The reporter may be asked questions during a live transmission, so you must be able to analyse the information you have and report your answers clearly and concisely in a way that both answers the question in the required time, and is also easily understood by the viewer or listener.

In a job such as assistant news editor, it is vitally important that you are able to work under extreme pressure, because you will have to solve problems quickly so that you are ready for transmission. You will also need to be able to check and edit reports for grammar, content, accuracy and conformity with house style.

A driving licence may be essential if working in local radio.

Jon Bithery
Broadcast journalism student, City University

I've always been a big fan of radio, and wanted to continue working in the medium on a more serious basis than I have been (so far I've just done deejaying on local commercial radio).

I worked as a newsreader at a station called Storm Digital, run by former Radio 1 DJ Bruno Brookes. I also worked on a freelance basis for a number of small stations including Mix 96 in Aylesbury and Kick FM in Newbury. I'm now working for LBC in London as a reporter on a part-time basis (i.e. when I'm not studying).

The course is a mixture of practical and theoretical work. The theory side of things includes lectures and seminars on journalism and society, and media law, whilst the practical side includes learning about how to write, put together radio reports and packages, develop interview techniques, and getting voice training. We have mock 'news days' where we run bulletins on the hour and a longer programme. We also run a proper FM radio station in the second term putting all these skills into practice. Two days in every fortnight are devoted to television; we use cameras to make films and then edit them. I chose to do the course because it's apparently got a very good reputation in the industry plus it's in central London thus giving good access to lots of juicy news stories!

Advice?
Just having a strong interest in the news and what's going on in the world around you. Definitely go for it if you're sure that it's what you want to do – but don't do it expecting fame or fortune!

PHOTOJOURNALISM/PRESS PHOTOGRAPHY

As a photojournalist or press photographer you will need excellent technical skills as well as qualifications and a good portfolio of work gleaned from work experience placements on local newspapers.

The NCTJ accredits courses in photojournalism and press photography or you may train for this certificate through a traineeship.

There is little room for error with press photography – even though every picture you see will have been digitally enhanced – so photographic skills are essential, including being able to recognise a good news picture when you see it.

Photographers may spend a lot of time waiting around, often in bad weather, for a newsworthy person to emerge from a building in order to capture the picture they need. It is therefore imperative that you have patience and the ability to remain calm, as well as speed and accuracy in getting your picture.

In recent years, members of the public have also provided photos of news events, sometimes taken on their mobile phones.

PICTURE RESEARCH

If you want to go into picture research, it goes without saying that you need to have good research skills, which can be demonstrated by an honours degree. Finding out the copyright ownership of a particular picture often takes a lot of detective work, as the picture may not be owned by the source you obtained it from.

You need to have visual flair, so that you can quickly decide which picture will fit the brief you have been given. Or you may have to commission a picture, so you need to be able to organise the shoot and all this entails. You will also need to be able to negotiate payment for the picture and/or photographer's fees, and you will have to work within budget.

Practical knowledge and experience, or even some qualifications in photography, are advisable, as is a course in picture research (contact the British Association of Picture Librarians and Agencies for course information – see Chapter 10 and Chapter 11).

It is also important to build up a contacts book of photographers, agencies, PR companies and so on, from any work experience you do or through your own detective work. Be aware of new photographers and go and visit as many exhibitions as you can, so you have a good knowledge of what is out there.

INTERNET

Journalists increasingly write for both print and the internet. In order to write for online publications you will need the necessary skills to write for the web. It is therefore likely that you will need to train in both print and online skills to increase your job prospects. You need to have knowledge and skills in HTML, Java and Perl.

Colin Meek
Freelance journalist

I did my degree in history followed by a postgraduate course in journalism at Cardiff University. After graduating I worked for the BMA (British Medical Association) *News Review* before becoming a consumer affairs journalist for *Which?* magazine. I then decided to go freelance, and have been for the past five years. I wanted to move away from London and live in the Highlands. I also work for dotjournalism. It covers very specific news targeted at journalists who work on the internet – using the internet either as a research tool or actually publishing on the internet.

No way could I work in the Highlands as a freelance journalist without the internet. The improvement in communication allows much more flexibility and much more freedom. I've used the internet for seven years, initially as a research tool. One of the dangers is the confusion between journalism and just publishing things on the web. There are very specific skills for journalists, whether they are working on the internet or on magazines or newspapers. Working on the internet is just another medium – you need 20% skills in understanding the internet and 80% journalism skills. The most important thing is to get the training in journalism then get the skills necessary to work online. Work for an internet publication and get the fundamental training.

Dotjournalism is the editorial arm of journalism.co.uk, a very good internet resource for journalists. Like most internet publications the idea was to publish a newsletter to encourage traffic to the site. It is now very successful with around 8,000 journalists subscribing.

I don't like sitting at a computer but the way I see it is that the internet should be saving you time. Used correctly, it should give journalists much more scope to become better informed and more tenacious. The internet journalism course at Preston is a good start. Journalism.co.uk is a huge and well-organised resource. People should also look to poynter.org in the US.

CHAPTER 6

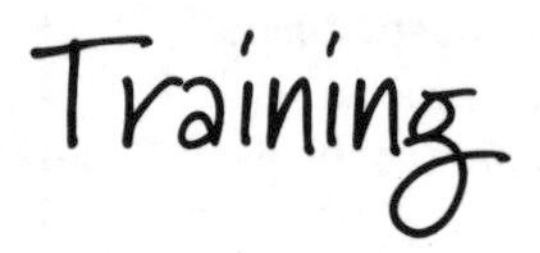

'Regional publishers invested £8.7 million in training, and 93% undertook training analysis.'

Newspaper Society

JARGON BUSTERS

- **NCTJ** National Council for the Training of Journalists
- **BJTC** Broadcast Journalism Training Council
- **PTC** Periodical Training Council. This is the training arm of the PPA (formerly known as the Periodical Publishers' Association)
- **Teeline** particular type of shorthand.

The type of training you receive to become a journalist is crucial. There are a whole variety of courses out there which offer journalism training, but is the one you're interested in recognised by the industry? There has been criticism from employers about the differing quality of journalism courses. A journalism course that is accredited by the NCTJ, PTC or BJTC will provide you with a qualification that proves you have the capabilities and skills to do the job.

With journalists at the heart of digital developments, it is only to be expected that journalism training must embrace these new challenges and opportunities. As a consequence, the NVQ training system for journalism has been merged with the NCTJ to create one vocational qualification for journalists, which will be administered by the NCTJ and will no longer be called an NVQ.

Whilst there is nothing wrong with taking a media-related first degree if that is your preference, a first degree in another area will be equally regarded and may be very relevant if you want to specialise in, for example, law or science. What is important is the quality of the degree, rather than the subject studied. You can always do a postgraduate qualification in journalism after you've graduated.

DEGREE RECOGNITION

Whatever media-related or journalism-related course you take, make sure it is one that is recognised and respected by the industry. Don't take a course that is trying to cash in on the level of demand for this type of training. Find out if the staff are currently working professionals. Are last year's students working, and where, and most important, is work experience a mandatory part of the course?

Speak to editors of magazines, newspapers etc. in the area that you are interested in, and ask their opinion about credible training.

Undergraduate courses normally last three years and postgraduate courses are usually one year. Fast-track postgraduate courses run for 18 to 20 weeks.

There are two routes into journalism: direct entry and pre-entry.

DIRECT ENTRY

When you enter the profession direct you are recruited to a trainee position straight from school or – much more likely – university, as a reporter or photographer (or similar level) by your employer, under the terms of a training contract. The training may be run in-house or you may be registered with a training organisation, typically the NCTJ, the BJTC or the PTC. The training usually lasts two years, the first six months of which are probationary (to see whether you've got what it takes to be a journalist).

The training will initially involve a distance learning foundation course. You will then attend a block-release or day-release course at college where you will have a series of seven preliminary exams to sit. After a further period of employment you will then have to prove your competence at the job in order to obtain your training organisation certificate.

Names and contact details of newspaper, magazine, television, radio and new media companies can be found in *Benn's Media Directory* and *Willing's Press Guide*, annual publications that can usually be found in the reference section of your local library. You can then apply direct to the publication or station you are interested in to see if they have any traineeship vacancies.

PRE-ENTRY

Pre-entry is when you study a full-time vocational course before entering the profession. These courses are open to people without a degree, although graduates stand a better chance of getting in. Make sure the vocational course you apply for includes a period of work experience, as this is probably the most valuable part of the course. You generally need to have undergone some relevant work experience just to get on to the course.

Even people who have completed a pre-entry course will enter the profession under an 18-month contract of training, with the first three months as the probationary period. You will also be expected to prove your competence by gaining a Level 4 qualification or equivalent at the end of this period.

NEWSPAPERS

There are various courses in newspaper journalism. All NCTJ (and equivalent) courses include law and public affairs. At the end of the training period you will need to prove your competence in newspaper journalism and be able to achieve shorthand at 100 wpm. Many local and regional newspaper groups, for example Trinity Mirror plc and the Midland News Association, run in-house training schemes, which are listed by the Newspaper Society. Contact the newspaper directly to find out if they are recruiting trainees, or check with your careers service. Some of these groups are listed in Chapter 10. Trainees will work on a variety of newspapers within the group and all areas of newspaper journalism will be covered. At the end of the training period you will attain a competence-based qualification.

National papers, such as the *Guardian* and *Daily Express*, often have graduate training schemes, as do press agencies such as Reuters. The demand for places far outweighs the number available, so expect competition to be extremely tough. Having relevant work experience with a portfolio of cuttings is vital.

MAGAZINES

There are a number of vocational courses in magazine journalism, some of which are accredited by the PTC or the NCTJ. The NCTJ courses cover news and feature writing, production and design, sub-editing, media law, ethics, government, shorthand to 80 wpm, and the background to the magazine industry. Results of preliminary exams will be assessed in conjunction with the portfolio of work that you have produced on the course.

Large, well-established magazine publishers such as IPC and EMAP offer in-house training schemes, but smaller publishers are less likely to do so. Contact the PTC for further information. In-house schemes will offer structured training in writing, reporting, proofreading, sub-editing, law, layout, design and production.

Dan Palmer
MA in newspaper journalism, Nottingham Trent University

I always enjoyed writing and I seemed to be quite good at it, so journalism seemed like a natural career choice. I also wanted to enjoy my job, and from all accounts journalism could provide that.

I am currently doing an MA in newspaper journalism; it's a one-year postgraduate course. The MA involves NCTJ qualifications such as law, public admin and shorthand, as well as newspaper training, where we learn to improve our writing skills. We produce one news story each week from a specific patch in Nottingham, and have also produced features, reviews and personal columns. On Friday we have a newsday, where between us we produce our own Nottingham-based paper.

The criteria I had to meet to be accepted onto the MA were a 2:1 degree, we also had to send some example work and complete a couple of news stories before being invited to an open day, where we did a general knowledge quiz, a couple more news stories, and an interview with the course leader.

I have not done any work experience but as part of the MA I will be on a work placement at the *Reading Evening Post*, *Portsmouth News* and the *Exeter Express and Echo*, a week for each.

The pros of the MA are it is definitely a great preview of life at a newspaper, the newsdays in particular are set up just like it would be at an actual paper. The course leader is a former journalist who knows the business and his input is valuable, he really tells us how to find the actual story in a piece of news, and my writing has come on no end. Can't really think of any cons!

When I complete my MA I hopefully will become employed at a newspaper.

Advice?
Study the courses carefully, there seemed to be a few 'journalism' MAs which appeared to have more to do with ethics and politics than actual writing whereas this course at Trent really prepares you for the industry. Look into the different areas of journalism, radio, TV, print etc, and choose a course that suits you.

BROADCAST JOURNALISM

Training for broadcast journalism covers basic journalism skills, but also teaches radio and television (bi-media) skills: many broadcast journalists start off at radio – generally local radio at first – and switch to television later as part of their career development. The television part of the training increasingly includes multi-skilling, as broadcast journalists may also be required to record their own broadcasts.

The BJTC ensures that colleges offering broadcast journalism courses meet industry standards by advising and assisting with the course syllabus. Colleges that meet and maintain the standards required by the BJTC will be granted accreditation. The BJTC courses cover technical skills and practical training in news writing, bulletin editing and interviewing techniques, law, public administration, local and central government, ethics and the media. The level of TV journalism studied varies from course to course but with the impact of the internet and the effect this has had on how news is delivered means that employers will be looking for a range of skills which reflects the growing trend towards multimedia. Many courses in broadcast journalism embrace these developments, so make sure you research the course you are interested in to find out if working across a range of platforms is included.

Some media companies offer in-house training, such as the BBC (which runs a News Sponsorship Scheme), ITN and Channel 4.

Courses may not always be regularly available, but are generally advertised in the press or on the company's own website.

In order to be considered for a trainee placement you must be a graduate, or – particularly for mature applicants – be able to prove a commitment to a career in broadcasting by having had relevant work experience.

Anila Khama
BA in broadcast journalism, Nottingham Trent University

It all started from my interest in media studies at GCSE level and then I went on to study A level media. I feel that my experiences in college had a great impact on my choice to go into journalism. As part of my enrichment activities I completed a year at a local radio station which gave me a taster of what the lifestyle of a journalist would be like. Then, in my second year, I worked on the college magazine, which I also enjoyed, and so it helped me to realise that journalism was the right path for me. A combination of my experiences and my characteristics made me choose journalism as I'm a nosey person who doesn't like to sit around. I like to keep updated on current affairs and at first the idea of investigative journalism was an added bonus to the other advantages of the field.

The name of my course is broadcast journalism and I am in my third and final year. The degree is purely based on journalism for broadcasting with a 50/50 split between TV and radio. Every year we have a law module which covers aspects of the law relating to journalists such as court reporting, defamation, contempt of court and freedom of information. The degree is advertised as being 50% academic and 50% practical and I've found this to be a true representation of how we are taught. We learn the practical side of journalism such as producing and reading radio bulletins and television news production through 'newsdays' that take place every week. This is where we all transform from students into professional, working journalists for the day with each person taking on a role.

We were expected to carry out some work experience as it was a requirement of a module in our second year. I completed this last summer at Heart 106 in Nottingham. I worked with a small news team helping them to produce copy stories, complete interviews over the phone and gain vox pops for a daily breakfast edition called 'Your Talk'. On the third and final week of my placement I moved on to completing full packages with a script for a reporter to voice. I thoroughly enjoyed my time at Heart 106 as it provided me with a fresh and slightly more interesting take on journalism with it being a commercial station. I have also worked as a runner on BBC's *The Big Questions* when they came to Nottingham for one show. This was not a requirement of my degree but I did come across the position through the course email system.

The criterion I needed to meet to get onto the course, if I remember correctly, was to have 300–340 UCAS points. But there would be some flexibility provided you could demonstrate an interest in news and current affairs through a short essay titled 'Why I want to be a broadcast journalist', along with a bulletin that we were told to read and submit on cassette.

The pros of the course have been meeting so many different people who are all interested in the same field as you and watch the news regularly; it makes you feel less geeky! Also the practical skills that will always stay with me as I now have the skills and confidence to apply for any broadcast or technical related position as well as journalism related vacancies.

On the other hand, it hasn't always been easy with the demanding hours and the need to switch from writing an academic dissertation to editing and interviewing people all over the UK for your feature. Juggling both the practical and written aspects of the course and fitting them into your timetable leaves you with almost no time to enjoy the other side of university life, so sometimes it would feel more like a job than a degree. Also, I was disheartened to learn that I'm more likely to report on garden sheds than to help uncover a major scandal.

When I graduate I would like to travel for about two months and earn some money part-time before I start working full-time as I do have fears of never getting the opportunity to travel again. Then towards the end of the summer I am hoping to secure a full-time job although I know it is so competitive – I have already started applying to television production houses and local commercial radio stations. I have a keen interest in working as a researcher in TV production or as a reporter for a commercial radio station. It's strange how they are both very different positions yet this course and my placement has opened up my options.

Advice?

My advice would be to get to know the industry, your interests within it and your own strengths and weaknesses. Once you have established them you will be able to pay extra attention to those weaknesses whilst on the course, even if this means devoting any spare time outside of university to this. For example, I had to work on my voice and tone to sound more authoritative. For those strengths I would recommend that you try and incorporate them into your work as it can pay off. If you have a passion for sports journalism or showbiz news make that clear in your application and demonstrate this through your work. Finally, show off your personality as it can be easy to fade into the background on such a course.

SPECIALIST JOURNALISM

If you are going to concentrate on a specific area, you will need specialist qualifications. It may be advisable to do a degree in your specialist area first, for example science, architecture or information technology. Alternatively, you will need to be able to demonstrate a strong passion for the subject.

If you are interested in becoming a science writer then you should look at doing a postgraduate degree in science and communications or a general journalism course. The Association of British Science Writers has information on courses and internships for work placements (see Chapter 11) and it could also be useful to contact the British Association for the Advancement of Science for advice.

If you are interested in fashion journalism, for example, you will not only need journalism skills and attributes, but must also have an ability to translate your knowledge and passion to the reader or listener, in a way that will both interest and inspire them. You will need to be able to predict trends before they break and give expert advice as to what looks good when and where. If you wish to specialise in fashion, the London College of Fashion offers various MAs and postgraduate certificates in fashion and lifestyle journalism.

New entrants to fashion are generally young (in their 20s) and may have completed a qualification in fashion and journalism. The College of Fashion offers a postgraduate course in fashion journalism. You should obviously target fashion magazines when applying for work experience placements.

The most popular areas, such as pop music and sport, are also the most competitive to get into. Specialist areas which are less competitive are easier to enter, as are trade and business magazines, so these should be targeted first.

There are various film journalism courses throughout the UK for those who wish to specialise in this very competitive field. Check out the British Film Institute website for further information.

Gabriel Green
Music Blogger, ICA Website

I got a job as an intern at the ICA through a photographer whom I was assisting. She had previously worked there and had recommended me to the music department for the internship. My job mainly entails photographing the gigs, collating and posting the blog and occasionally writing the gig reviews. I also do three days a week in the office helping the music head with emails/bookings/organising/copy and during our own nights help to look after the artists.

I think writing a blog is a slightly more personal style than other forms of writing – you are relaying your experience to the reader rather than just the information.

I spent a year and a half studying for a photographic BA at the London College of Communication (LCC – formerly known as the London College of Printing) before leaving due to dissatisfaction with the course. Then I got a job in a photo studio and proceeded to manage the studio for two years before working full-time assisting a photographer. Other than the music blog I do have a photoblog.

I think digital media is extremely important – it is a natural evolution that has greater accessibility, although it lacks the tactile quality and tradition of newspapers/magazines etc. I think there is space and necessity for both.

Alyson Rudd
Football reporter and sports columnist for *The Times*

My job entails going to see premiership matches, cup matches or European matches. When I go to see a typical evening match during the week I take my computer along, and write as the match is going. The writing is very adrenaline-driven and exciting. The paper needs the copy in the office as the match finishes to send to far-flung corners of Britain. I send the first 500 words by the end of half time and then another chunk three-quarters of the way through and any extra items on the final whistle at the end of play. It's very intense. If the computer goes or the link to the office gets broken it is very scary.

After the match I go to the press conference and interview the managers, then rewrite the copy with quotes from the managers and make it a proper story. It is all done at pace and you feel completely exhausted. Sometimes it is very cold too.

The Saturday match is much more relaxed. I watch the whole match and work afterwards, putting in fresh quotes for the Monday paper. There is a separate press conference by the managers for the Monday papers. I write up this piece on Sunday and I won't mention the match very much but take a different angle on the story. That's why I really like writing for daily papers, because you have the contrast of the relaxed Saturday match and the fast-paced evening match, which are two very different styles.

My first paid journalism job was at this fashion house, and I don't know why I ended up there. Then I got a job working for the *Pharmaceutical Journal*, this was back in the days when I literally had to paste copy in by hand. I did lots of proofreading of very long pharmaceutical words. Then I got a job as a financial journalist, even though I hadn't done any writing.

I decided to move over to writing about football because at the trade magazines I wasn't writing anything I was passionate about. But no one was taking risks; you have to prove you can work for a national paper, so I devised a plan. Mine is a very unusual route. The *Observer* was running a charity auction and one of the prizes was to meet the Liverpool team, the team I support. So I thought if I could meet them I could write a piece about them and try and get the paper interested. My friend Sue and I bid £400 (this was in 1992 so quite a lot of money) and we won, so I phoned the *Observer*. The sports editor wouldn't touch it, but the features editor was interested and they sent along a photographer. So I wrote the piece and sent it in. I sent the published piece to the *Independent* and they gave me four Sunday columns in the *Independent on Sunday*, on sport. Then I sent all of this to *The Times*, who tried me out on some Saturday football matches They were pleased with my piece and invited me into the office to say well done. They gave me more and more work so I eventually gave up my financial job.

Advice?

It depends what you are doing at the moment. Get involved in writing up sports events and be involved in sports. If you're not a player, get involved in the administrative side, get involved somewhere and never turn down any job that has any connection with sport. The sports editor doesn't want someone who is picky. If you're lucky you'll be a given a match to see how you get on. You won't get much money, probably just enough to cover your expenses. But you might be at the right match when something happens and you'll be able to make a name for yourself. I know someone who sent in a letter to a national paper. The paper suddenly needed someone in Norwich four hours before a match because the journalist who was supposed to cover it was ill. The sports editor remembered receiving a letter from someone in Norwich and so this guy got the job – just from one letter. He eventually got a full-time position. Always grab your opportunities.

PHOTOJOURNALISM AND PRESS PHOTOGRAPHY

The photojournalism course covers all the elements of a journalism course, including reporting, but with photography as its foundation. You will develop a natural news sense combined with an ability to use a camera and the relevant equipment.

Training in press photography is the same as the photojournalism course but without the reporter's module. After the completion of a successful period of employment, most companies will award the NCTJ's national certificate in photojournalism/press photography.

Courses in photojournalism and press photography are available at Sheffield College, Norton, University College Falmouth, London College of Communication and the University of Gloucester.

Leon Neal
Photojournalism student, Sheffield College, Norton

The course covers all aspects of photojournalism, ranging from traditional developing and theory to 'paparazzi' and riot training. I can't think of any other course where you learn so many varied things. In one day, you can take lessons on caption writing, newspaper practice and how to use your camera as a defensive weapon! The course lasts for under a year when taking the pre-entry course. For professionals who already work in the industry but need to gain the knowledge, it can be completed in block form, which lasts 12 weeks and is very intensive. At the end of the course, the student is expected to find a place of work and get hands-on experience for a year or so before returning to college to take their final NCE exams. If they pass, they are now classed as a senior photographer and can expect higher pay and better jobs.

After my GCSEs, I took A levels in Psychology and English Literature (which I didn't do too well in), but also completed a foundation course in journalism. This really gave me a deeper interest in the news and its coverage. It was only due to a lack of funds to pay the course fees that I did not carry straight on to attend the NCTJ course at 18 years old.

I completed a period of work experience at the *Sheffield Star*, which was a valuable chance to see what work was like in the real world. Despite the course doing everything it can to recreate what it's like, actual experience is vital. The first time I had the responsibility of arranging and shooting a group of strangers for the *Star* was certainly strange. I kept having out of body thoughts about 'Why the hell aren't they taking any notice of me? I've no idea how to do this!' Obviously, this was just first-time nerves as the shoot came together, the picture editor liked the shots and they were published the next day. It was a great feeling to know that all the readers would be seeing my shots.

I have found the whole course to be a challenging and inspiring experience. Before I decided to come back into education, my life had not been moving that fast. The thrill of having creative work to do every day, while learning new skills and abilities has been incredible.

The biggest downside is the time element. My girlfriend has seen less and less of me since the course started and it will soon get to the point where I have to leave Sheffield, my girlfriend, my house and my friends. A tough time indeed, but I feel that staying in Sheffield would mean I never get to really push myself to see what I can do. It's not a choice I really want to make but it's a necessity.

Advice?
Give it a go, but be aware of the commitment you will have to make to get anywhere. Learn as much about the world as you can to increase your general knowledge. It really is helpful to have a basic understanding of politics, current affairs and history. Attending courses such as the NCTJ is a great way to learn as it gives you a chance to try your hand at the profession in a friendly environment. It's fine to make and learn from your mistakes at college before you enter the industry, so take advantage of it.

PICTURE RESEARCHERS

Postgraduate diplomas or masters are available in publishing, but picture research is rarely an important part of the syllabus, so you may need to take a short course in picture research.

The London School of Publishing has a 10-week course in the subject, and the Publishing Training Centre at Book House has a one-day course and a distance-learning course.

COURSES

COURSES ACCREDITED BY THE NCTJ

Institutions accredited by the NCTJ must adhere to a very strict set of guidelines. The whole of the NCTJ's syllabus must be taught, and regular inspections are undertaken to ensure that high standards are maintained.

The NCTJ has two levels of qualification for reporters – the preliminary exams and the National Certificate Examination (NCE). Online journalism already features in the NCE and is being integrated into all courses, including an optional video element at preliminary level (in a portfolio of work, not an exam).

Institutions that currently offer courses accredited by the NCTJ are listed below. All courses are in newspaper journalism unless otherwise stated. Courses do not always begin at the start of the academic year. Please check with the individual institution or with the NCTJ.

Institution	Course
Bournemouth University	BA (hons) in Journalism
Brighton Journalist Works	12-week Diploma in Production Journalism plus two-week Certificate in Sub-editing*
Brunel University	MA in Journalism
Cardiff University	PgDip in Newspaper Journalism
Cardonald College, Glasgow	HND in Journalism Studies
	Day release – Newspaper Journalism
City College Brighton and Hove	Fast-track PgDip in Newspaper Journalism
	Academic year course in Newspaper Journalism
	Day release – Newspaper Journalism
City of Wolverhampton College	Foundation Degree in Newspaper Journalism
Cornwall College Camborne	Fast-track course in Newspaper Journalism
Darlington College of Technology	Fast-track course in Newspaper Journalism
	Block release in Newspaper Journalism
De Montfort University	PgDip in Newspaper Journalism
Edge Hill University	Degree
Glasgow Caledonian University	BA (hons) in Journalism
Harlow College	Fast-track PgDip in Magazine Journalism
	Academic year course in Magazine Journalism
	Academic year course in Newspaper Journalism
	PG in Newspaper Journalism
Highbury College, Portsmouth	(Fast-track in Newspaper Journalism)
	One year part-time in Newspaper Journalism
	Block release in Newspaper Journalism

Institution	Course
Kingston University	MA/PgDip in Journalism
Lambeth College	PG fast-track in Newspaper Journalism
Leeds Trinity & All Saints College	Foundation degree in Journalism
	MA/PgDip in Print Journalism
Liverpool Community College	Fast-track PgDip in Newspaper Journalism
	Fast-track PgDip in Magazine Journalism
	Academic year course in Newspaper Journalism
	Day release in Newspaper Journalism
Liverpool John Moores University	BA (hons) Journalism
Midland News Association	Midland News Association training scheme
News Associates/Sportsbeat	Fast-track in Newspaper Journalism (sport option)
	Part-time course in Journalism
noSweat journalism training, London	Part-time course in Newspaper Journalism
	Fast-track in Newspaper Journalism
Nottingham Trent University	BA (hons) in Print Journalism
	MA/PgDip in Newspaper Journalism
Press Association Training	Editorial Foundation Course in Newspaper Journalism
Sheffield College, Norton	Academic year course in Newspaper Journalism
	PG fast-track in Newspaper Journalism
	Academic year course in Press Photography or Photojournalism
	12-week block release in Press Photography
	12-week block release in Photography
Staffordshire University	BA (hons) in Journalism (sport option)

(Continued on the following page)

Institution	Course
Sutton Coldfield College	Pre-entry course in Newspaper Journalism
University of Brighton	BA (hons) in Sport Journalism
University of Central Lancashire	BA (hons) in Journalism
	PgDip/MA in Newspaper Journalism
	MA in Magazine Journalism
University of Cumbria	BA (hons) in Journalism
University of Kent	BA (hons) in Journalism and the News Industry
University of Portsmouth	BA in Journalism (combined honours)
University of Salford	BA Journalism (combined honours)
	MA PgDip in Journalism
University of Sheffield	BA in Journalism (single and combined honours)
	MA in Newspaper Journalism
University of Sunderland	BA (hons) in News Journalism
	BA (hons) in Magazine Journalism
	BA (hons) in Sports Journalism
	MA in Newspaper Journalism
University of Teesside	BA (hons) in Multimedia Journalism Professional Practice
University of Ulster	MA in Newspaper Journalism
Up to Speed Journalism Training Ltd	Fast-track in Newspaper Journalism
Warwickshire College	Pre-entry (academic year) course in Newspaper Journalism

***Note:** although there is only one centre that an NCTJ-accredited sub-editing course is offered, there are several accredited newspaper courses which offer an additional certificate in sub-editing. These courses are available at:

- Cardiff University
- Cardonald College
- De Montfort University
- Edge Hill University
- Harlow College
- Highbury College
- noSweat
- Portsmouth University
- News Associates/Sportsbeat
- Sunderland University
- Staffordshire University.

At the time of writing, some courses were not yet fully accredited. Please check with the NCTJ for further information.

The NCTJ also offers seven distance-learning courses in the areas below.

Main courses

- Foundation course in news reporting
- Writing for the periodical press
- Basics of sub-editing.

Short courses

- Media law
- Introduction to local government
- Introduction to central government
- Introduction to newspaper law.

Certification is awarded on successful completion of exams.

You are advised to take the online self-test in order to establish the course suitability.

Short training courses are also offered in London or in-house by the NCTJ, but these are aimed at people already working in the industry.

COURSES ACCREDITED BY THE PTC

The PTC accredits colleges that provide the quality training required by the magazine and professional media industry. PTC-accredited courses provide you with an approved industry-recognised qualification. Courses may also include other related areas of media training such as newspaper, broadcast or online journalism, but it is paramount that they cover magazine journalism in order to be PTC accredited. Courses with current accreditation are listed below.

Institution	Subject	Type of course	Course length
Bournemouth University	Multimedia Journalism	BA (hons)	3 years
Cardiff University	Journalism Studies	Postgraduate Diploma	9 months
City University	Magazine Journalism	Postgraduate Diploma	1 year
Goldsmiths College	Journalism	MA	1 year
Harlow College	Journalism Studies	BA	3 years
	Magazine Journalism	Postgraduate	19 weeks
Highbury College	Magazine Journalism	Pre-entry Diploma	23 weeks
PMA Training	Magazine Journalism	Postgraduate	9 weeks
Sheffield University	Journalism Studies	BA	3 years
Southampton Solent University	Journalism	BA (hons)	3 years
University College Falmouth	Journalism	BA (hons)	3 years
University of Central Lancashire	Journalism	MA	1 year
University of Westminster	Periodical Journalism	Postgraduate Diploma	1 year

COURSES RECOGNISED BY THE BJTC

Courses in broadcast journalism are now increasingly available and the BJTC now accredits nearly 50 of them with several more courses pending their recognition. Below is a list of courses currently accredited by the BJTC. Contact the individual institutions for further details about the courses they offer.

Institution	Course
Birmingham City University	MA/PgDip in Broadcast Journalism
Cardiff University	PgDip in Journalism Studies
City University	MA/PgDip in Broadcast Journalism
	MA/PgDip in TV Current Affairs Broadcast Journalism
Goldsmiths University	MA in Radio
	MA in TV Journalism Radio
Highbury College, Portsmouth	PgDip in Broadcast Journalism
Leeds University	BA (hons) Broadcast Journalism
National Broadcasting School, Brighton	NBS Diploma in Broadcast Journalism
Nottingham Trent University	BA (hons) Broadcast Journalism
	MA/PgDip in Online Journalism
	MA/PgDip in Radio Journalism
	MA/PgDip in TV Journalism
Sheffield University	BA (hons) Broadcast Journalism
	MA/PgDip in Broadcast Journalism
	MA/PgDip in Web Journalism
Southampton Solent University	BA (hons) in Journalism
Staffordshire University	BA (hons) Broadcast Journalism
	MA/PgDip in Sports Broadcast Journalism
	MA/PgDip in Broadcast Journalism
Trinity and All Saints, Leeds	MA/PgDip in Bi-media Journalism
	MA/PgDip in Radio Journalism
University of Bournemouth	BA (hons) in Multimedia Journalism
	MA in Multimedia Journalism
	BA (hons) in Multimedia Journalism
University College of Creative Arts	BA (hons) in Journalism
University College, Falmouth	MA International Journalism (broadcast pathway)

(Continued on the following page)

Institution	Course
University College, Falmouth	MA/PgDip in Bi-media Broadcast Journalism
	BA (hons) Journalism
University of Central Lancashire	MA/PgDip in Broadcast Journalism
	MA/PgDip in Online Journalism
University of Cumbria	BA (hons) Journalism
University of Gloucester	BA (hons) Broadcast Journalism
University of Lincoln	BA (hons) in Journalism
University of Ulster	MA Journalism (broadcast pathway)
University of the West of Scotland	Graduate Diploma in Broadcast Journalism
University of Westminster	MA/PgDip in Broadcast Journalism

Courses which are pending accreditation are at the following institutions:

- University of Sunderland
- University of Winchester
- University of Glamorgan
- Napier University, Edinburgh
- Glasgow Caledonian University
- University of Wolverhampton.

If you are interested in studying at any of the above universities, check and find out when accreditation is likely.

Many courses, but not all, now include online skills training. Always check the course content for further information.

FUNDING

It is very difficult to get funding for courses in journalism, but bursaries are available, often for specific institutions. The following organisations may be able to help if you fit the necessary criteria.

The NCTJ administers bursaries for people from ethnically and socially diverse backgrounds who are doing an NCTJ accredited course through its Journalism Diversity Fund. Visit www.journalismdiversityfund.com for further details.

The Leach Trust has established a bursary scheme that will enable three graduates with disabilities to study for a one-year postgraduate course in broadcast production or broadcast/print journalism.

The NUJ has set up the George Viner Memorial Fund to encourage British Black and Asian students who want to take industry-recognised pre-entry courses but lack the money to do so.

For further information on the above bursaries and other sources of funding, check out the NUJ website.

CHAPTER 7

Work experience

The news that citizen journalists write about has a number of different outlets, including blogs, user comments (attached to news stories), images, video footage taken from personal mobile phones, independent and collaborative news websites, emailing newsletters and personal broadcasting sites. There is now even a citizen journalism channel on YouTube. These are all routes for you to try and get your work published to provide you with a portfolio of work.

GETTING YOUR WORK PUBLISHED

Keep up to date with what's happening on the web and initiate contact with publishing sites which you personally enjoy and feel have a good future. Send in articles which may be chosen for publication in local papers or ezines. For example, surreal comedians, The Mighty Boosh, publish *Cheekbone*, which is an online magazine entirely written and photographed by Boosh fans. Getting any of your work published anywhere helps to build up your portfolio.

Check out websites such as www.theonlines.co.uk, which is specifically for citizen journalists to contribute articles. For photojournalists there is www.planetpaparazzi.com. Most

BROOKLANDS COLLEGE LIBRARY
WEYBRIDGE SURREY KT13 8TT

newspaper websites advertise contributors' guides with contact details. If you want to try and contribute your work, consider which section of the website you should target, then contact that section's commissioning editor with a brief outline of your idea. If you're lucky, your work may be checked out, although this doesn't mean it will be used, but if it does get published you may even get paid.

In 2004, associatedcontent.com, a citizen journalism website, was launched, describing itself as the 'People's Media Company'. This was the first company to pay users for any content (articles, videos and audio clips) published on the site. Submitting work to an online publisher such as this could be a good way of having evidence of work experience and getting paid for it too!

WORK EXPERIENCE

Work experience can be part of a journalism course. On some courses you will be given placements, and on others it is up to you to find the work experience opportunities.

You can start by getting work experience on your student paper, magazine or website, or on hospital radio. You could even set up your own ezine with the help of like-minded people. This kind of work experience will stand you in good stead if you then try for work placements at the local newspaper or radio station.

Larger magazines and regional or national newspapers or radio stations will be inundated with applications, so competition for work placements is fierce. If you want to get work experience on a magazine, it is worth applying to smaller titles, where the competition will not be so great, and you may have more opportunity to do proper work. The PPA has information on organisations that offer work experience. It is worth applying to magazines that deal with a topic or hobby that you are particularly interested in.

It is highly unlikely that you will end up becoming employed by the company that you do your work experience for, but it does happen occasionally. Whatever the outcome, work experience is vital to gaining future employment. It not only demonstrates your commitment to the industry and helps you build up your list of contacts, but it also gives you the necessary experience of working in a real-life situation, which all counts when compiling your CV.

If you want to get into picture research you could apply to local libraries, picture libraries, or magazines or newspapers, where you could work on the picture desk. You might get the opportunity to assist on a picture research job, and that will help you develop a book of contacts. The British Association of Picture Libraries and Agencies has a register of people looking for work experience.

Wherever you end up getting work experience you will undoubtedly do some tasks that won't be relevant to learning the skills of journalism, like filing or making tea – this is all part of the deal. But whatever you do, whenever an opportunity arises to do some background research, prepare for an interview, or even write or take photographs, be sure to grab it and show everybody how talented you are. You can always offer your opinions and ideas. If they are good enough, you will get noticed, and you may even get something published, or better still, be offered some paid work. Make sure you listen to any advice you are given and ask questions, but don't harass staff, especially when they are working under extreme pressure as a deadline approaches.

If you get some work published or presented, you may be paid for it, but don't always expect to be. According to the NUJ, any published work should be paid at the normal rate. However, even if you don't get paid you will have your name in print and a cutting to put in your portfolio of work.

Most people look for work placements as the academic term ends in June or July. To increase your chances of getting a placement, try and apply at other times of the year when there is less demand.

The BBC offers a wide range of opportunities for work experience and you can browse their full range of short unpaid journalism placements on their website. Be warned, this is a national company so competition is extremely tough. Television, in general, is tough to get into, as it is a relatively small but highly popular industry.

Elizabeth Gobeski
Intern, *Earthmatters*

I first became interested in journalism when I took a journalism course in my junior year of high school. I took the course just because it sounded easy, but once I began to see how much a journalist can effect change, I really fell in love with the subject.

My training has not been very formal. I took a year-long course covering the basics of journalistic writing in my junior year of high school. The next year I worked as editor-in-chief of my high-school newspaper, editing and laying out stories. In my second year of college I took another year-long journalism course, but this didn't cover anything I hadn't already learned in high school. After that I worked as features editor of my university paper. It's unfortunate that I haven't had more formal training but such courses simply aren't offered at my university; that said, I've learned most of what I know just from reading newspapers and magazines on a regular basis.

I worked as an intern for *Earthmatters* for two and a half months. The job entailed a lot of proofing as well as some subbing. I also wrote quite a few NIBs (news in briefs). These were 50–150-word pieces. My proofing and subbing skills certainly improved and writing NIBs forced me to learn how to relay important information in a very short space. It gave me an appreciation of how important every sentence is in a news piece – there's no room for irrelevant facts or presumptuous language in *Earthmatters*.

Advice?
Attend a university that has a well-respected journalism programme. Having had almost no formal journalistic training it was extremely difficult for me to find any kind of internship/placement.

APPLICATIONS AND INTERVIEWS

When you apply, include a concise, grammatically accurate and well-written CV, which should be no longer than one or two sides of A4. The CV should be tailored to the newspaper, magazine, radio or website you are applying to. You will need to show evidence of your commitment to journalism by listing any work you have had published or broadcast.

If you are applying for work experience, the company you are applying to won't expect a front-page, eight-column news item from *The Times*, but they will want to see a film review you did for your university magazine or website or hear a recorded news item you did for your college radio.

If it is a job or course you are applying for, you will be expected to provide relevant work experience on a local paper or radio station or trade magazine. An application supported by cuttings and/or pictures makes it easier for the commissioning editor to assess your worth.

You will need to include a covering letter or email to accompany your CV and cuttings or tape. Always find the name of the person you need to write to. Tell them what you want to do, what you can offer and your motivations for applying. Convince them that you are worth taking on. To do this you must show you have read the magazine or paper or seen the programme, looked at back issues, are aware of its style and content and the direction that it is moving in. You can also suggest new ideas or ways of developing current ones. Above all, the letter must be an interesting read and well written: if it isn't, how can you expect to make a career in journalism?

If you are invited for an interview, you can really show your knowledge of the title or programme by discussing its attributes and target audience, and offer ideas in keeping with its remit. Make sure you are fully prepared and able to answer questions about the company, and about the competition too. Don't forget, the main purpose of the interview is to find out more about you as a person, so be friendly, passionate and positive: if you are not, even if you have good qualifications, they won't be interested.

If you get a work placement, use it to find out about all areas of the publication or programme. Ask for advice on how you can improve your role. Keep a list of the new contacts you are making. Afterwards, write and thank the person who arranged the placement and the people you worked with. If you did your job well and made an impression, the chances are they will remember you if a suitable vacancy should arise.

Do expect some rejections, but don't let these put you off. One of the best attributes of a good journalist is persistence, which you will need in abundance just trying to break into the industry. If you really want to make journalism your career, with hard work and determination you will.

CHAPTER 8

Competitions and awards

Entering competitions, and there are tons out there, can help you to focus your work and to gain an understanding of what you are up against. If you are talented enough to win an award, you will gain prestige and it will be a very helpful addition to your CV. Some competitions include the prize of a short working contract, which will give you a good way of entering the profession and plenty of work experience to help develop your career.

There are several awards for journalists, some of which are included below. If you think your standard is good enough and if you meet the criteria needed to enter the competition, give it a go – what have you got to lose?

The Association of Photographers (AOP) has a number of photographic awards including the Assistants and Student Photography Award. The International Digital Exhibition and Awards (IDEA) were also originated by the AOP.

FASCINATING FACT

The *Press Gazette*, a UK trade magazine, was the first to honour the best citizen journalist with the Citizen Journalism Award.

The BJTC holds an annual Young Broadcast Journalists of the Year Award in radio journalism and television journalism. The awards are open only to students on courses accredited by the BJTC and entrants must be in their final year or on a postgraduate course. This is to ensure the student's most mature work is put forward.

The Guardian Student Media Awards has categories for journalists, editors and photographic students. Prizes include cash, work experience at *The Guardian* and Sky News, and air flights. Categories of the year include: student newspaper; student magazine; student reporter; student feature writer; student photographer; student publication design; student website; student critic; small budget publication; student sports writer; student diversity writer; student travel writer and student columnist.

London Press Club Award has the following categories: scoop of the year; business journalist of the year; Edgar Wallace Award for fine writing, and new media journalist of the year.

Oneworld Media Awards has several categories, including radio news award, women's achievement award, next generation award and new media award.

The *Press Gazette* Regional Awards include: young journalist of the year; reporter of the year; photographer of the year; sports photographer of the year; and the online news service award. They also have a Student Journalism Award which is open to anyone who has or was studying at any academic level during the previous 12 months to be a journalist of any discipline; print, broadcast or online.

The Times and Tabasco annually award the Young Photographer of the Year prize.

Lizzie Hosking
Junior writer, *New Woman*

I started off doing a month's work experience at *Elle* magazine in April 2001. They asked me to stay on in an unpaid work experience basis, so I quit university and stayed on (and got a £10,000 bank loan to support myself, which I'll be paying back forever!). I was there until December that year, when I got the job of editorial assistant on *New Woman*, which was just next door. I've been here since.

Work experience was my training. It really is the most important thing, not that courses aren't beneficial – they are – but getting your face known and being in the right place is a huge help. I've been getting work experience since I was about 14, on local papers and college papers, and then at the *Mail on Sunday* and so on. Getting work experience is really hard these days, though. I used to write about 10 letters a week and had three rejections from *Elle* before they took me on!

To get the job in the first place you need to be determined and really, really want to do it – the money isn't that great even when you finally do get a job so, if your heart's not in it, you're better off getting a well-paid job that you're not really into instead! You definitely need the ability to get on with people. Oh, and when it's print week you'll probably be working late every night – you've got to not mind that!

A good editorial assistant must be someone who's unflappable, can do a million things at once, has the ability to prioritise (because you'll get a million things thrown at you at once and every one is a priority) and is organised.

Advice?
Work experience, work experience, work experience!

CHAPTER 9

The review: a round-up

You've got the passion, you've got the determination and you've got the get up and go. Now go out there and get yourself experienced. Take any placement that offers you the chance to learn new skills, develop your writing and/or photography and get the best thing of all – seeing your name in print.

- Keep a **list of contacts** of the people you work with or for. Maintain these contacts – talk to them, ask them questions, find out about opportunities for placements or traineeships and network.

- Get your **qualifications** – if you want to specialise in a particular subject make sure you study for this at first degree and at postgraduate level if necessary. Do a pre-entry course in journalism or try the direct entry route and get a traineeship. Make sure you continue to get work experience while studying. Make sure any course you undertake is respected and recognised by the industry.

- Keep all your cuttings in a **portfolio** or **showreel** as applicable.

- Keep an eye on the relevant trade journals, national media press and the internet so you keep **up to date** and are **knowledgeable** about the industry. **Read** as much as you can – books, directories, magazines, ezines, websites and so on – and join organisations if you think they will be of benefit. **Talk** to people already working in the industry, particularly someone who is doing the job you would ultimately like to do.

- Many journalism unions and **organisations** offer free student membership, which is a useful means of getting to know more about the industry.
- Send **speculative letters** to all the media you would like to work for. Tell them what you can do, what you want to do and your motivations.
- Write a punchy **CV** that markets you in the best possible way. Tailor your CV to the job you are applying for, or the publication or programme if applying on spec.
- If you find an opening, make sure you **read the publication or website** or **watch/listen to the programme**. Find out everything there is to know about it, including who their market is, what their house style is like, which direction they're going in and who the competition is. Come up with brilliant ideas that fit into the publication/programmes remit and will separate you from the next wannabe journo.
- Maintain your **enthusiasm**. Don't let rejections put you off. Keep a flexible approach.

So what are you waiting for? Get out there and do it.

Alan Morrison
Reviews editor, *Empire*

Aside from the reviewing that I do as a writer, my full-time job at *Empire* is to be in charge of the 'Reviews' section – i.e. all the 'opinion' in the magazine, be it new films, DVDs, books, soundtracks. I start a production period by compiling a list of

what's going to be coming out (in cinemas or into the shops) in a given month. This info comes from press releases sent in, research done on several internet sites selling DVDs and, mostly, by phoning the film distribution companies and press agencies. When I've got a finished list, I draft a page plan – looking at the number of pages I'll need in the magazine to cover all these releases, then breaking down each page into larger and smaller reviews depending on what I think will be the interest to the readers/scale of release/quality of the film. That's usually about 12 or 13 pages for new films in the cinema and a total of about 35 pages for DVDs, videos, books, etc. Then comes the real skill of the section editor: matching the right person to the right film.

Although the section is a collection of individual voices giving their subjective views, I try to establish a more objective '*Empire*ness' overall, so that while some readers come to trust and appreciate some writers more than others, it is *Empire*'s opinion that counts. I approach either staff members or a team of freelance reviewers and commission them to do reviews by sending them to an advance press screening or sending them an early copy of a DVD. I give them word counts and deadlines, making sure that I can get all the elements on any single page back to me at around the same time, so I can then send completed pages to our art editor for design. When the reviews are sent to me (by email) I check over them, polishing a sentence here and there just to establish a standard house style.

I was brought on board at *Empire* because I had a wide knowledge and taste in films, so very much part of the job of sorting out the section comes down to me mixing new commercial movies with good cult titles, world cinema and classic oldies to highlight the best of what's out there each month. I guess that's my interest/knowledge in this area. Films have always been my hobby, but I love all kinds of cinema – and as the magazine caters to film fans of all tastes, the reviews editor should have as wide a taste and knowledge as possible.

I have no formal journalistic training, and most of the people I know working in arts journalism don't have any either. It's very much viewed as something that's useful for news reporting. But if you're going to specialise in any of the arts (or, I suppose, in fashion or anything like that), knowledge/contacts/writing ability take precedence. The further you rise up the editorial ladder, the more experience takes over from any training qualifications.

Advice?

It's partly 'right place, right time', but you've got to have the ability to back that up if an opening appears. Sometimes the best writer in the world will get knocked back time and time again simply because this arts/entertainment sphere is totally oversubscribed. Most people get an editorial position by being a writer first of all, but then showing a good deal of dependability and calm-headed organisational skills. Work experience is the way in. It gives you an idea of what working in this environment really entails – you'll see the 80% slog/20% fun split first hand. If you get a work-experience week, the balance is to not get in the way, but still be noticed. If it's film you're into, volunteer to work at the closest film festival to you as a) you'll see films not yet released and can perhaps get someone to take a review from you when the film is due to come out; and b) you'll make contacts with journalists and press officers attending.

Always tailor reviews you're sending in to the style of that publication, even if it means rewriting every application: 1,200 words on your favourite movie is no use if that publication never runs anything longer than 400 words. Follow their layout: is it one continuous piece, or is a synopsis of the film lifted out separately and a final summary opinion their particular style? Don't worry if you don't have published clippings: a skilled sub-editor might have rewritten your piece before it was published, for all we know. Your own raw opinions, if they're impressive enough, will showcase your views and writing style. Oh, and pay particular attention to the first line of a review: if that doesn't catch the reader's attention, they won't go on with the piece.

CHAPTER 10

Organisations

Below is a list of useful organisations. They all have websites to visit for further information, many with lots of useful advice, contacts and links. Full contact details can be found in Chapter 11.

GENERAL

ASSOCIATION OF BRITISH SCIENCE WRITERS (ABSW)

The ABSW publishes the *Science Reporter* for its members and produces a leaflet, 'So you want to be a science writer'. It also organises events and functions, and provides information on bursaries and awards, including the Medical Journalism Awards.

ASSOCIATION OF PHOTOGRAPHERS (AOP)

The AOP is for photographers and photographers' assistants in fashion, advertising and editorial. Its aim is to protect their rights and promote their work. It is a non-profit trade association with a membership of over 1,800. It is affiliated to a number of colleges and promotes the relationship between these colleges and the industry, giving students the opportunity to gain experience in the workplace. The AOP is establishing a worldwide network of photographers and image-makers, and it provides information, education programmes, exhibitions, publications, awards and careers advice.

BRITISH ASSOCIATION OF PICTURE LIBRARIANS AND AGENCIES (BAPLA)

BAPLA is the trade association for picture libraries in the UK, with over 400 UK picture library members it is the largest organisation of its kind in the world. Its website covers: what is a picture library?; copyright and licensing; using a picture library; submitting pictures to a library; vacancies; image/contact search; events and publications and jobs.

BRITISH INTERNET PUBLISHERS ALLIANCE (BIPA)

The BIPA promotes the growth and development of new internet services in a way that allows a wide diversity of entrants to the market on a free and fair competitive basis. BIPA has grown rapidly in size and influence in the last five years.

BRITISH RESEARCH AND DATA (BRAD)

Updated information on over 13,500 media entries across all sectors. Figures for circulation and audience reach allow you to make comparisons between titles.

BROADCAST JOURNALISM TRAINING COUNCIL (BJTC)

A partnership of the main employers in the UK broadcasting industry: the BBC, ITV News Group, ITN/IRN, Channel 4, BSkyB, Commercial Radio Companies Association, Sky News, Reuters, GCAP Media News, Radio Centre, NUJ and Skillset, plus colleges and universities whose courses it accredits. Associate members comprise nearly 30 colleges and universities, and nearly 50 courses, training new generations of broadcasting journalism talent.

GUILD OF REGIONAL FILM WRITERS

The guild hosts three 'Cinema days' weekends at different locations nationwide to preview films and provides opportunities for a range of interviews to be conducted with film-makers, actors and writers. Membership of the guild includes journalists, broadcasters, distributors, film programmers and festival directors.

JOURNALISM.CO.UK

This website, run by journalists, contains a database of job vacancies. Subscribers can have job vacancies emailed to them.

The website also has a database of freelance journalists, runs a free daily news service dedicated to online journalists, editor's blog, and contains information on training events, journalism awards and relevant links.

JOURNOLIST

An annotated list of sites chosen to help reporters, writers and editors make good use of the internet. This site provides a quick guide to the basics for journalists who have not been trained to work online. The links lead to pages about the different ways you can use the internet in journalism. It also provides information on the following search areas: general information on a subject; specific documents; news stories happening now; archive or current output of news organisations; email mailing lists or email magazines; reference material usually based on printed sources; finding specific people; who owns websites and email addresses; 'invisible' or 'hidden' web. www.journolist.com.

NEWSPAPER SOCIETY

The society is a source of comprehensive information on regional and local newspapers in the UK. It includes information on ownership of titles, circulation details and contact information at publishing group, centre and individual newspaper level (for example, Office for National Statistics link, lists of relevant libraries as well as experts who may be prepared to be interviewed on specific subjects). The society provides advice for would-be journalists and takes a leading role in the continuous development of professional qualifications in newspaper journalism. Membership is open to UK newspaper companies. Non-membership services include courses in media and editorial law.

ONLINE CONTENT UK

Organisation and community for editorial professionals. Members range from webeditors to content producers. The website lists information on events and jobs.

PICTURE RESEARCH ASSOCIATION (PRA)

Professional organisation for picture researchers, picture editors and anyone involved in the research, management and supply of visual material to the media industries. Website includes information, vacancies, freelance register, careers information, courses, advice, *Montage Magazine* journal, *The Bulletin* (bi-monthly news digest) and events. The PRA has drawn up a standard freelance engagement contract for members to use if they wish. *Picture Research in a Digital Age*, an ebook by Julian Jackson, looks at time-saving tips for the picture researcher faced with technology.

PPA

The PPA is the association for publishers and providers of consumer, customer and business media in the UK. PPA members produce over 4,500 products. The Periodical Training Centre is the training arm of the PPA.

PRESS COMPLAINTS COMMISSION

An independent, self-regulating body that deals with complaints regarding the editorial content of newspapers and magazines.

PROSPECTS

Prospects is the official graduate career website. It includes careers advice, jobs, further study, company profiles, work experience and your university careers service.

PUBLISHING TRAINING CENTRE AT BOOK HOUSE

Open courses include editorial, electronic publishing, journals, publishing, computing and rights and contract. Distance learning courses and online training are also available.

RESEARCHBUZZ

News about search engines, databases and other information collections.

SCOTTISH NEWSPAPER PUBLISHERS ASSOCIATION (SNPA)

Represents the publishers of 100 weekly and bi-weekly newspapers as well as 30 free newspapers. It promotes the 'Scottish Weekly Press' and offers a number of services.

SKILLSET – SECTOR SKILLS COUNCIL FOR THE AUDIO-VISUAL AND PUBLISHING INDUSTRIES

Skillset's mission is to raise skills levels to meet the needs of the audio-visual and publishing industries, including developing qualifications that meet industry needs. It provides impartial careers advice online, face-to-face and over the phone. Its website carries information on careers, training, standards, qualifications and funding.

UK ASSOCATION OF ONLINE PUBLISHERS (UKAOP)

The UKAOP presents a unified voice to industry and government, specifically to address issues and concerns relating to all areas of online publishing.

EMPLOYERS

There are many more employers than those listed below. You can find information about other employers from relevant directories or some of the organisations listed above.

AGENCE FRANCE PRESSE (AFP)

AFP provides a photo service, general news wires and business and sports news. It is the world's oldest established news agency and continues to expand its operations worldwide with thousands of radio, television, newspaper and company subscribers. Its worldwide network covers 165 countries, with 2,900 staff and stringers. Coverage is organised around five regions: North America, Latin America, Asia–Pacific, Europe–Africa and the Middle East.

AFP News Online is a specially crafted real-time news service for websites. AFP 'à la carte' is worldwide news delivered direct to your email address.

ARCHANT

Archant is the UK's largest independently owned regional media business. It is active in regional newspapers and magazine publishing, contract printing and internet communications. It has 2,600 employees and Archant Regional, its newspaper division, is one of the UK's top five regional newspaper publishers. The website contains job vacancies.

ASSOCIATED PRESS

Founded in 1848, the Associated Press is the oldest and largest news organisation in the world, serving as a source of news, photos, graphics, audio and video for more than a billion people every day. It has 243 bureaus in 97 countries worldwide; 1,700 US daily, weekly, non-English and college newspapers; with 5,000 radio and television outlets taking the Associated Press. AP uses five languages (English, German, Dutch, French and Spanish) and the reports are translated into many more languages by international subscribers. The Associated Press employs 4,100 editorial, communication and administration staff worldwide, 3,000 of which are journalists. News is reported 24 hours a day, seven days a week.

BBC

The BBC runs some professional training schemes that have a very good reputation. Competition for places is very fierce and only a few places are available. There is no guarantee that the schemes will always run. The BBC also offers work-experience placements. Job vacancies and trainee placements can be viewed on its website.

DAILY MAIL AND GENERAL TRUST (DMGT) PLC

DMGT is one of the largest international media companies in the UK and has interests in national newspapers and related digital operations, and in local radio, business and financial information and exhibitions.

EMAP COMMUNICATIONS

EMAP Communications is a B2B media group. It's leading publications include *Retail Week* and *Broadcast*. In March 2008, EMAP plc was acquired by Eden Bidco, a joint venture between investors APAX and Guardian Media Group.

GUARDIAN MEDIA GROUP

One of the UK's leading multimedia companies. Its diverse portfolio includes Guardian News and Media, GMG Regional Media, GMG Radio and Trader Media Group.

HAYMARKET PUBLISHING LTD

Haymarket publishes a number of leading UK titles in consumer, business and customer media, for example *Conference*, *Incentive Travel*, *Marketing Event* and *Campaign*.

HAYTERS TEAMWORK

The leading editorial sports agency in the UK. The agency is always happy to be contacted by talented, young sportswriters who have completed the NCTJ training course and have at least a year's newspaper agency experience.

IPC MEDIA

IPC is the leading UK consumer magazine publisher. It has a diverse print and digital portfolio including *What's on TV* and nme.com. IPC's five core markets are: TV; women; men's lifestyle and entertainment; home and garden; and leisure. IPC publications reach over 70% of women, 50% of men and more than 60% of the online population.

JOHNSTON PRESS PLC

Johnston Press is a major publisher of local newspapers and internet sites, basing its publishing philosophy on local service to local communities. It has over 140 markets from St Andrews to Portsmouth and its publications and internet sites are tailored to their local area. It is currently the third largest publisher of local and regional newspapers in the UK and hosts a lot of local internet sites. Its website includes a company directory, job vacancies and annual reports.

MEDIA NETWORK

The Media Network specialises in UK-wide journalism and media recruitment for print, new media and corporate communications.

MIDLAND NEWS ASSOCIATION

The Midland News Association publishes regional and local newspapers in the West Midlands as well as owning four radio stations. Its two regional evening papers are the *Express and Star* and *Shropshire Star*.

NATIONAL ASSOCIATION OF PRESS AGENCIES (NAPA)

NAPA's freelance journalist and photographer members are among the most productive in the UK. It has members working for the top agencies in the country, covering every town and city of the British Isles.

NEWS CORPORATION

Diversified entertainment company with operations in eight industry segments: film and entertainment; TV; cable network programming; direct broadcast; satellite TV; magazines and inserts; newspapers and information services; and book publishing. It creates and distributes English language news, sports and entertainment around the world. It has operations in the UK, Australia, continental Europe, Asia, the Pacific basin and the USA. The company publishes more than 175 different newspapers, employs approximately 15,000 people worldwide and prints more than 40 million papers a week. HarperCollins is its publishing division.

NEWSQUEST

Newsquest, a subsidiary of Gannet Company Inc, is a leading publisher of regional and local newspapers, magazines and websites. Newspapers include the *Northern Echo* (Darlington), the *Telegraph and Argus* (Bradford) and the *Argus* (Brighton). The group has almost 300 weekly newspapers and 17 dailies, with a weekly circulation of more than 10 million, and about 8,500 employees. It also has a network of more than 180 local newspaper and portal websites. Newsquest also produces a portfolio of niche magazines and supplements. Its website includes information on jobs and contacts.

NORTHCLIFFE MEDIA

This is one of the largest regional newspaper publishers in the UK, operating from 39 publishing centres. Its daily titles have a combined sale of almost one million copies per day and its online 'This is' network attracts around one million users monthly. It produces many thousands of different publications for companies and organisations including local and central government, charities, radio stations, television companies etc. Harmsworth Printing (formerly the Northcliffe Press) provides a unique and comprehensive print and publishing service to businesses and organisations across the UK and Eire.

PRESS ASSOCIATION

The Press Association is the national news agency for the UK and Ireland providing news 24 hours a day, 365 days a year to every national and regional daily newspaper, the major broadcasters, online publishers and a variety of commercial organisations. The

Press Association has a network of news and sports reporters, photographers and video journalists around the UK and in key locations internationally, covering all major breaking stories.

TRINITY MIRROR

Trinity Mirror was the result of the merger in 1999 of Trinity plc and Mirror Group plc. It publishes 150 regional newspapers, five national newspapers and over 200 websites.

UK PUBLISHING MEDIA ALLIANCE

A £22 billion-alliance of newspapers, magazines, books, journals and data publishers. The alliance is made up of the Newspaper Publishers' Association, the Newspaper Society, the Publishers Association and PPA.

UNITED PRESS INTERNATIONAL

The newspaper publisher, United Press International, began as a company by combining three regional news services to form the United Press Association, based on the principle that there should be no restriction on who could buy news from a news service.

CHAPTER 11

Useful contacts

REFERENCE BOOKS

Benn's Media Directory – Hollis Publishing Ltd
Dod's Parliamentary Companion – political reference book, Dod's Parliamentary Communications
Media 08 – The essential guide to the changing media landscape, Guardian Newspapers Ltd
The Picture Researcher's Handbook – PIRA International Ltd
Who's Who in the Media – Guardian Newspapers Ltd
Willing's Press Guide – Romeike Research Ltd
Writers' and Artists' Yearbook – A&C Black Ltd
The Writer's Handbook – Bramley Books

NEWSPAPERS, MAGAZINES, BULLETINS, NEWSLETTERS, EZINES AND WEBSITES

Audit Bureau of Circulation www.abc.org.uk
British Journal of Photography
Broadcast – weekly, EMAP Media Ltd
Campaign – weekly, Haymarket Publishing Ltd
dotjournalism – online news for online journalists, Mousetrap Media www.journalism.co.uk

Digital Media news for Europe – www.dmeurope.com
Financial Times, Financial Times Group
freelanceuk.com
freelance-writers.co.uk
Guardian, Guardian Newspapers Ltd
guardianunlimited.co.uk – archive search, arts, books, business, editorial, film, football, jobs, media, money, *Observer* online, politics, shopping, society, sport, talk, travel, UK news and world news.
grfw.co.uk Guild of Regional Film Writers
holdthefrontpage.co.uk
ifreelance.com – advertise your journalistic skills online and bid for job offers
Image
Independent Newspaper Publishing plc
Institute of Interactive Journalism – j-lab.org
journolist – www.journolist.com
journalism.co.uk
journalismuk – provides an essential directory of links for journalists.
mediaguardian.co.uk
mediatel.co.uk – planning and research information for all media genres, MediaTel Group
Media UK – internet directory listing of all online UK media, Media UK
Media Week – weekly, Quantum Publishing
mediaweek.co.uk
mediamoves
New Media Age – for new media news
Online Content UK – www.onlinecontentuk.org
The Photographer
planetpaparazzi.com – citizen photo journalism website
ppajobs.co.uk – lists vacancies for magazines and media jobs online
Press Gazette – Quantum Publishing www.pressgazette.co.uk
prospects.ac.uk – graduate recruitment
publishingmedia.org.uk
Radio Magazine – Goldcrest Broadcasting Ltd
researchbuzz.org
Telegraph – www.telegraph.co.uk
The Times – Times Newspapers Ltd
Times Online – www.timesonline.co.uk
theonlines.co.uk – UK website for citizen journalists

thepapr.com – American website for citizen journalists
Trotman websites – careers A–Z
UK Publishing Media Alliance www.publishingmedia.org.uk

ORGANISATIONS

Association of British Science Writers (ABSW)
Wellcome Wolfson Building
165 Queen's Gate
London SW7 5HD
Tel: 0870 770 3361
Fax: 020 7973 3051
Email: absw@absw.org.uk
Website www.absw.org.uk

Association of Photographers (AOP)
Wellcome Wolfson Building
165 Queen's Gate
London SW7 5HD
Tel: 0870 770 7101
Fax: 0870 770 7102
Email: info@the-ba.net
Website: www.the-aop.org

British Association for the Advancement of Science
The BA
23 Savile Row
London W1S 2EZ
Tel: 020 7973 3500
Fax: 020 7973 3051
Email: help@the-ba.net
Website: www.the-ba.net

British Association of Picture Libraries and Agencies (BAPLA)
18 Vine Hill
London EC1R 5DZ
Tel: 020 7713 1780
Fax: 020 7713 1211
Email: enquiries@bapla.org.uk
Website: www.bapla.org.uk

British Internet Publishers' Alliance (BIPA)
Website: www.bipa.co.uk

British Library Newspaper Library
Colindale Avenue
London NW9 5HE
Tel: 020 7412 7353
Fax: 020 7412 7379
Email: newspaper@bl.uk
Website: www.bl.uk/collections/newspapers

British Research and Data (BRAD)
Insight
Greater London House
Hampstead Road
London NW1 7EJ
Tel: 020 7728 4390
Fax: 020 7728 4800
Email: sales@bradinsight.com
Website: www.intelligencia.com

Broadcast Journalism Training Council (BJTC)
18 Miller's Close
Rippingale
nr Bourne
Lincolnshire PE10 0TH
Tel: 01778 440025
Email: sec@bjtc.org.uk
Website: www.bjtc.org.uk

National Council for the Training of Journalists, NCTJ Training Ltd
The New Granary
Station Road
Newport
Saffron Walden
Essex CB11 3PL
Tel: 01799 544014
Fax: 01799 544015
Email: info@nctj.com
Website: www.nctj.com

National Union of Journalists (NUJ)
308 Gray's Inn Road
London WC1X 8DP
Tel: 020 7278 7916
Fax: 020 7837 8143
Email: info@nuj.org.uk
Website: www.nuj.org.uk

Newspaper Society
St Andrew's House
18–20 St Andrew Street
London EC4A 3AY
Tel: 020 7632 7400
Fax: 020 7632 7401
Email: ns@newspapersoc.org.uk
Website: www.newspapersoc.org.uk

Periodicals Training Council
PPA
Queens House
28 Kingsway
London WC2B 6JR
Tel: 020 7404 4166
Fax: 020 7404 4167
Email: deborah.oliver@ppa.co.uk
Website: www.ppa.co.uk/ptc

Photo Imaging Council (PIC)
Orbital House
85 Croydon Road
Cateham
Surrey CR3 6PD
Tel: 01883 334497
Fax: 01883 334490
Email: pic@admin.co.uk
Website: www.pic.uk.net

Picture Research Association
c/o 1 Willow Court, off Willow St
London EC2A 4QB
Tel: 020 7739 8544
Fax: 020 7782 0011
Website: www.picture-research.org.uk

Press Complaints Commission (PCC)
Halton House
20–23 Holborn
London EC1N 2JD
Tel: 020 7831 0022; helpline 020 7353 1248
Fax: 020 7831 0025
Email: complaints@pcc.org.uk
Website: www.pcc.org.uk

Publishers' Association
29B Montague Street
London WC1B 5BH
Tel: 020 7691 9191
Fax: 020 7691 9199
Email: mail@publishers.org.uk
Website: www.publishers.org.uk

Publishing Training Centre at Book House
45 East Hill
London SW18 2QZ
Tel: 020 8874 2718
Fax: 020 8870 8985
Email: publishing.training@bookhouse.co.uk
Website: www.train4publishing.co.uk

Skillset: Sector Skills Council for the Audio Visual Industries
Focus Point
21 Caledonian Road
London N1 9GB
Tel: 020 7713 9800
Fax: 020 7713 9801
Email: info@skillset.org
Website: www.skillset.org

Scottish Newspaper Publishers' Association (SNPA)
48 Palmerston Place
Edinburgh EH12 5DE
Tel: 0131 220 4353
Fax: 0131 220 4344
Email: info@snpa.org.uk
Website: www.snpa.org.uk

Skillset Careers (specialist media careers advice)
Skillset Focus Point 21 Caledonian Rd.
London N1 9 GB
Tel: 020 7713 9800
Website: www.skillset.org.uk

Society for Editors and Proofreaders
Erico House
93–99 Upper Richmond Road
London SW15 2TG
Tel: 020 8785 5617
Fax: 020 8785 5618
Email: administration@sfep.org.uk
Website: www.sfep.org.uk

The Media Network
28 Mortimer Street
London W1W 7RD
Tel: 020 7637 9227
Fax: 020 7323 3903
Email: across@tmn.co.uk
Website: www.tmn.co.uk

UK Association of Online Publishers
Queen's House
55–56 Lincoln's Inn Fields
London WC2A 3LJ
Tel: 020 7404 4166
Fax: 020 7404 41697
Email: info@ukaop.org.uk
Website: www.ukaop.org.uk

USEFUL ADDRESSES

Agence France Presse
3rd Floor 78 Fleet St.
London ECAY INB
Tel: 0207 353 7461
Email: contact@afp.com
Website: www.afp.com/english/home/

Archant
Prospect House
Rouen Road
Norwich NR1 1RE
Tel: 01603 7727772
Website: www.archant.co.uk

Associated Newspapers (publishes *Daily Mail*, *Mail on Sunday*, *Evening Standard*)
Northcliffe House
2 Derry Street
London W8 5TT
Tel: 020 7938 6000
Fax: 020 7937 4463
Website: www.associatednewspapers.com

Associated Press
International Headquarters
450 W 33rd St
New York NY 10001
Tel: (001) 212 621 1500
Website: www.ap.org

Association of Publishing Agencies (APA) (representative body for customer magazine publishers under the PPA)
Queens House
3rd Floor 55/56
Lincoln's Inn Fields
London WC2A 3LJ
Tel: 0207 404 4166
Website: www.apa.co.uk

BBC
Website: www.bbc.co.uk

Daily Express
Express Newspapers
Website: www.express.co.uk

Daily Mail and General Trust plc
Website: www.dmgt.co.uk

EMAP Ltd
Northcliffe House
Derry Street
London W8 5TT
Tel: 020 7938 6000
Website: www.emap.com

Guardian Media Group
60 Farringdon Road
London EC1R 3GA
Tel: 020 7278 2332
Fax: 020 7242 0679
Email: contact@guardian.co.uk
Website: www.gmgplc.co.uk

Haymarket Media Group
Website: www.haymarketpublishing.co.uk

Hayters Teamwork
Image House
Station Road
London N17 9LR
Tel: 020 8808 3300
Fax: 020 8808 1122
Email: info@haytersteamwork.com

IPC Media Ltd
Blue Fin Building
110 Southwark Street
London SE1 0SU
Tel: 0870 4445000
Website: www.ipcmedia.com

Independent Television News (ITN)
200 Gray's Inn Road
London WC1X 8XZ
Tel: 020 7833 3000
Fax: 020 7430 4305
Website: www.itn.co.uk

Johnston Press plc
Tel: 0131 225 3361
Website: www.johnstonpress.co.uk

London School of Publishing
David Game House
69 Notting Hill Gate
London W11 3JS
Tel: 020 7221 3399
Fax: 020 7243 1730.
Email: lsp@easynet.co.uk
Website: www.publishing-school.co.uk

Midland News Association
51–53 Queen Street
Wolverhampton W1V 1ES
Tel: 01902 313131
Email: wolverhampton@expressandstar.co.uk
Website: www.expressandstar.co.uk

National Association of Press Agencies
c/o Mercury Press Agency
Unit 218
Century Buildings
Tower Street
Liverpool L3 4BJ
Website: www.napa.org.uk

News Corporation
Website: www.newscorp.com

Newsquest Media Group Website
www.newsquest.co.uk

Northcliffe Media Ltd
Tel: 020 7400 1401
Website: www.dmgt.co.uk/corporatestructure.northcliffemedia

Press Association
292 Vauxhall Bridge Road
London SW1V 1AE
Tel: 0870 120 3200
Website: www.pressassociation.co.uk

Prospects CSU (UK's official graduate careers website)
Prospects House
Booth Street East
Manchester M13 9EP
Website: www.prospects.ac.uk

Radar
The Disability Network
12 City Forum
250 City Road
London EC1V 8AF
Tel: 020 7250 3222
Fax: 020 7250 0212
Minicom: 020 7250 4119
Email: radar@radar.org.uk
Website: www.radar.org.uk

Reuters
Website: www.reuters.com

Scottish Newspapers Publishers Association (SNPA)
48 Palmerston Place
Edinburgh EH12 5DE
Tel: 0131 220 4353
Fax: 0131 220 4344
Email: info@snpa.org.uk
Website: www.snpa.org.uk

Trinity Mirror Plc
1 Canada Square
Canary Wharf
London E14 5AP
Tel: 020 7293 3000
Website: www.trinitymirror.com

United Press International
Website: www.upi.com